Gender Roles

Independence
Educational Publishers
Cambridge

First published by Independence
PO Box 295
Cambridge CB1 3XP
England

British Library Cataloguing in Publication Data
Gender Roles – (Issues Series)
I. Donnellan, Craig II. Series
331.1'33

ISBN 1 86168 154 2

Printed in Great Britain
The Burlington Press
Cambridge

Typeset by
Claire Boyd

Cover
The illustration on the front cover is by
Pumpkin House.

CONTENTS

Introduction

Gender Roles is the eighteenth volume in the **Issues** series. The aim of this series is to offer up-to-date information about important issues in our world.

Gender Roles looks at sexual equality in school, in the home and in the workplace.

The information comes from a wide variety of sources and includes:
Government reports and statistics
Newspaper reports and features
Magazine articles and surveys
Literature from lobby groups
and charitable organisations.

It is hoped that, as you read about the many aspects of the issues explored in this book, you will critically evaluate the information presented. It is important that you decide whether you are being presented with facts or opinions. Does the writer give a biased or an unbiased report? If an opinion is being expressed, do you agree with the writer?

Gender Roles offers a useful starting-point for those who need convenient access to information about the many issues involved. However, it is only a starting-point. At the back of the book is a list of organisations which you may want to contact for further information.

*****

Equality issues in education

Information from the Equal Opportunities Commission

Admission

Schools cannot refuse admission to a prospective pupil on the ground of their sex, or to try to maintain a gender balance by admitting one sex but not another when places are limited. In the private sector, if tests are used as part of a screening or selection process, girls and boys must sit identical tests, and the calculation of scores must not be based on the use of different exam norms.

Curriculum

Girls and boys must have precisely the same access to the curriculum. That is, exactly the same amount of subject teaching and the same subject options. Most schools start with this premise, but also aim to ensure a broad and balanced curriculum. A good curriculum is relevant to all pupils; it reflects diversity and cultural heritage; it builds in positive images and positive action to ensure equality of opportunity is met. Time-tables can be structured in such a way that real choice exists.

The hidden curriculum

Children learn a great deal at school and not just from formal classroom lessons. What they see around them teaches them as well. Images and pictures in books and on walls; who does what in the school; rules and regulations give clear messages. For example, if all the books are about boys having adventures and girls doing the washing up this does not provide good role models or a real picture of what life is really like. Thankfully there is a much wider choice of books now available in schools which provide a more stimulating selection to the young reader. There are many ways in which, often unintentionally, differences based on gender can lead to different treatment. This can give

EQUAL
OPPORTUNITIES
COMMISSION

the wrong signals about what girls or boys can achieve. Teachers and parents should not expect different behaviour or achievement from girls or boys. Girls should not be expected to be quieter or better behaved than boys. It must not be assumed that boys can make more demands on a teacher's time.

Careers guidance

Pupils should have equal access to course option consultation and careers guidance, and the counselling offered must not be discriminatory. Girls and boys should be made aware of the full range of options available and be encouraged to participate in the broad range of work experiences on offer. Furthermore, pupils should be positively encouraged beyond conventional choices. Positive images such as girls in technology should be used to encourage others. Similarly, boys that choose modern languages, home economics or secretarial studies should not be deflected by sexist assumptions. They should also be encouraged without bias. Pupils should not be given the impression that there are 'jobs for men and jobs for women', but should be encouraged to make subject choices and follow career paths which interest them and correspond with their talents. Careers advice and literature must not differentiate between 'male' and 'female' employment. This is important, not only because girls should not be discouraged from many excellent career opportunities in an increasingly

technological society, but also because boys will find that many of the jobs traditionally done by men no longer exist, or are few in number. Effective, non-restrictive course options and careers guidance can expand opportunities, give more young people access to economic ladders and widen opportunities for personal development.

Pastoral care and personal and social development

Pastoral care in schools provides for the emotional, physical and social needs of individual pupils. All adults in a school should work to foster the belief that all people have value in their own right, and to create a non-threatening atmosphere that encourages co-operation. Guidance staff offer support to all pupils, within their remit, both individually and in groups, and focus particularly on pupils who are socially or emotionally needy or at risk, and those who have encountered discrimination or harassment.

Personal and Social Development (PSD) is a planned programme carried out in secondary schools, aimed at helping pupils to develop positive attitudes and personal and social skills. PSD courses are built on the principles of equality, justice and mutual respect, and focus on issues such as:

- challenging stereotyped assumptions
- raising self-esteem
- fostering positive relationships
- promoting cultural identity
- acting independently and decision making
- taking responsibility for one's actions
- working with others
- leadership.

Discipline

Not only should the disciplinary policy be the same for both sexes, but the same standards should be expected of girls and boys. Responses to disruptive behaviour should be free of bias, and reactions to disruptive behaviour based on stereotypical images should be discouraged. For example, a pupil should not be reprimanded for behaving in what is perceived to be

an 'unfeminine' or 'unmasculine' way. If behaviour is praiseworthy or unacceptable, this should be decided regardless of the pupil's sex.

Language

Language, spoken as well as written, is a powerful means of reinforcing or developing attitudes, and consideration should be given to the language used in teaching. The use of gender-dependent words such as headmaster rather than head teacher should be avoided, and attempts should be made to find gender-neutral words, especially when defining occupations, for example, fire-fighter, police officer. The use of sexist terms should be discouraged. The school's discipline policy should make it clear that sexist language which uses gender as a form of abuse will not be tolerated.

Teaching materials

All pupils should have unbiased access to school resources and teaching materials. These materials should avoid the depiction of adults in traditional stereotypical roles, and males and females should be equally represented in textbooks, posters and other visual aids. These should represent all sections of society and challenge prejudice, injustice, racist and sexist views. With regard to school equipment, research has suggested that boys dominate the use of equipment in science, technology, design and computer studies. Practices must therefore be in place to ensure that both sexes receive equal hands-on experience.

Accommodation and facilities

Accommodation and facilities provided in school must take account of all pupils. Classrooms should be

safe and stimulating places for everyone. They should also be organised so as to present a welcoming aspect to both sexes. This is particularly important in the areas of science and technology where in the past a 'macho' image or ethos may have been created which was off-putting to many girls. A contrasting environment may have been created in other subject areas such as Home Economics, with similar results for boys. Just as teaching materials should be widely representative of society, the school environment as a whole should portray positive images of all members of society, especially those who are often portrayed negatively, and should challenge stereotypes.

Dress/uniform

Requiring girls and boys to wear separate school uniforms may be in breach of the Sex Discrimination Act. School uniform has tended in the past to be based on male norms, for example the wearing of ties has been expected of both boys and girls. Recent attempts to modernise uniform have favoured a unisex approach with sweatshirts as an alternative. Schools might wish, however, to adopt a less prescriptive approach: if it is simply made clear that pupils are expected to dress in a way that is appropriate, safe and practical, some of the confrontation arising in this sensitive area might be averted.

Extra-curricular activities and sports

Girls and boys must have the same access to all extra-curricular and out-of-school activities, such as chess clubs, hockey clubs or theatre visits. Single-sex competitions in sports are permitted where physical differences between the sexes could disadvantage women or girls. In some schools this has provided legal support for continuing to divide girls and boys into sporting activities traditional to their sex. There is strong evidence, however, that many pupils at both primary and secondary levels are eager and able to participate in a full range of sports, not just in single-sex teams but also in mixed competitive events.

The Equal Opportunities Commission (EOC) believes it is wrong that girls who are fit and able to participate in a sport, and capable on their merits to play on teams, should be banned from taking part in the activities they choose. Girls should have the same right as boys to develop their skills. Sport is now the only area of the school curriculum where equality of opportunity is not always provided.

Bullying and harassment

Sexual harassment is not defined in the Sex Discrimination Act, but it can be described as unwanted physical or verbal abuse of a sexual nature which adversely affects an individual. The EOC believes that the Sex Discrimination Act extends the unlawful nature of sexual harassment to the field of education. This would mean that an education authority would discriminate against a girl or boy if they did not take steps to prevent the sexual harassment of pupils by teachers.

Bullying and harassment in schools most often occurs when a pupil becomes a victim of other pupils. Bullying of this kind tends to arise from sexual stereotyping of the worst kind, and is based on the popular notions of 'acceptable' male or female behaviour. Boys and girls whose appearance or behaviour does not conform to popular myths are often cruelly victimised by their peers. Schools should ensure that their Equal Opportunities and Bullying Policies make it clear that such behaviour will not be tolerated. Coercion, however, is ineffective if unsupported by good practice. If schools continue to do as much as possible to generate an unbiased culture of mutual respect, it is hoped that incidences of bullying and sexual harassment will decrease, and that, as pupils progress into the adult world, society itself will gradually be influenced in its thinking.

Assessment

Procedures for classroom testing and assessment must not discriminate against pupils on the ground of sex. Girls and boys should be set the same tests, and different sex norms must not be used in the calculation of the test score.

Early intervention

Parents know that children's attitudes are formed at an early age, and their perceptions about gender are no exception. A recent study of six- and ten-year-olds found that 70 per cent of six-year-old boys wanted to be sportsmen, especially footballers; this rose to 85 per cent by the age of ten. As for girls, 40 per cent of the six-year-olds wanted to be nurses and 30 per cent teachers; at ten years of age roughly one-third wanted to be teachers and the remainder were divided between being flight attendants and hairdressers. Those working with pre-school children should therefore be as vigilant as primary and secondary school staff regarding the provision of a discrimination-free environment in terms of play, books, materials and resources.

Differences between girls and boys in educational outcomes

Sex stereotyping still has a strong influence on course choices made by pupils: greater numbers of boys take technological and scientific subjects, while girls dominate in English and modern languages. Given the present skills shortages in the areas of science, technology and information technology, and the growing importance of language skills, it is important that both girls and boys are encouraged into those areas of future employment.

In addition to different academic outcomes, there are disparities in personal development. Some girls leave school with low self-esteem and low expectations. Many boys, on the other hand, leave school inadequately prepared for the expression of their feelings, for the building of personal relationships and for the acceptance and enjoyment of family responsibilities. Once again, these differences can be addressed by tackling inherent attitudes to gender roles. Only by changing traditional attitudes to 'male' and 'female' areas of the curriculum and by making these equally attractive to both sexes, will real equality be achieved.

For further information

The above information is an extract from *An Equal Opportunities Guide for Parents* and is available free of charge from the EOC web site at www.eoc.org.uk or you can write to them at Equal Opportunities Commission, Scotland, St Stephens House, 279 Bath Street, Glasgow G2 4JL. Tel: 0141 248 5833. E-mail: scotland@eos.org.uk

© Equal Opportunities Commission (EOC)

Pupils achieving 5 or more GCSE grades A*-C

Girls' examination performance has improved over time and they now outperform boys. In 1998/99, 53 per cent of girls aged 16 achieved five or more grades A to C at GCSE or SCE Standard grade compared with 42 per cent of boys.

Boys | Girls

	1990/91	1993/94	1995/96	1996/97	1997/98	1998/99
Boys	36.0%	39.0%	39.9%	40.5%	41.3%	42.6%
Girls	44.0%	48.0%	49.4%	50.0%	51.5%	53.2%

Source: Department for Education and Employment (DfEE). © Crown Copyright

Young women and education

The situation at European level

Education has long been perceived as an essential vehicle of equality between women and men. The availability of secondary school for all children, with more democratic access to university, has changed the lives of many individuals, in particular women, and led to a more open society in Europe.

Education and training are vital for developing equal opportunities throughout our society. If education systems do not challenge traditional stereotypes on the role of women and men in our society, those stereotypes will continue to have a damaging influence. Education and training also constitute some of the main instruments in today's changing world in helping young people to face the challenge of increasing internationalisation and globalisation:

- Across the European Union, 110 women for 100 men have higher education qualifications, while at general upper secondary level, 124 girls obtain qualifications for every 100 boys.
- Studies have shown that teachers in general give more time and attention to boys than to girls in mixed classes and that girls do better in maths and science in girls-only classes.
- While the educational attainment of women is outstripping that of men, this is not reflected in the employment situation of women. The unemployment rate of women in the EU (approximately 12%) is higher than that of men (9%).
- Concerning the participation of women in initial vocational education and training, there is still a male dominance of about 55 per cent men to 45 per cent women across the EU.
- Women are seriously under-represented in scientific fields. They only account for 25 per cent

of students in science and technology subjects. In engineering, they account for 6 per cent of students.
- Very few of them are appointed to university chairs or research teams. The proportion of female full professors ranges from 4% in Austria to 13.8% in France.

These situations are not merely discrimination. It is also a loss for European society as a whole, which is depriving itself of the intellectual potential of half of its population at a time when it has to compete in the global market.

Young women make the majority of university students now in most of the Member States of the European Union, but their type of education and studies are normally the ones that present the highest rates of unemployment.

Teachers in lower education are mainly women but when it comes to higher education the percentage of women teachers declines.

Traditionally ethnic minority groups place great faith in education as a way to improve their long-term situation in society, believing that education will provide them with opportunities to succeed on their own merit. But parents of young migrant or ethnic minority girls have to face serious lack of information about the functioning of the education systems. In some ethnic minority communities the education of girls is not seen as a priority and they are neither encouraged nor supported to pursue higher education. In fact, in some cases, they are actively prevented from doing so. The access to education of these young women is therefore even more difficult.

Disabled women need specific measures to overcome barriers to access the education systems. They

may need special education systems, methods or physical spaces. These range from adequate facilities to special educational systems.

What can be done?

There is still much to change and a lot of governmental policies must be influenced by an equality and gender vision.

Our aims should be to:

- Promote gender equality in schools towards pupils as well as towards teachers, education staff and parents and in education materials, which often carries stereotypes.
- Encourage gender equality in careers advice.
- Encourage gender equality in teacher training and integrate gender equality as a cross-cutting theme in all compulsory academic curriculum.
- Promote a greater participation of women in committees, assemblies, and advisory groups assisting the Commission in the implementation of possible initiatives at EU level to engage the Commission for the promotion for women in science.
- Promote a significant participation of women in scientific events such as conferences and workshops.
- Promote the use of a neutral and non-sexist language. Each language has many examples that should be added in each case.
- Education in sexual equality should be included in all educational materials.
- Need of gender sensitive statistics on the situation in universities in the EU.
- Introduction of compulsory courses of women's history in secondary education.

The above information is from the European Women's Lobby's web site which can be found at www.womenlobby.org

© European Women's Lobby (EWL)

Girls take top grades in most subjects

First detailed GCSE breakdown confirms trend that puts girls on top and leaves boys best only in mathematics

By Rebecca Smithers, Education Correspondent

Girls are outperforming boys both at the top grades and across subjects, it was confirmed last night after the publication of the first GCSE results broken down by gender.

Even in mathematics – the only subject where boys won more A* grades than girls – achievement by the two sexes was broadly the same, the exam boards said.

The joint council for general qualifications last night published details of examination results on behalf of the regional boards not only for GCSEs, but also for GCSE short courses, certificates of achievement and the vocational part one, and foundation and intermediate GNVQs.

The figures confirmed that youngsters took more exams than the previous year – the number of GCSE entries increased by 5.4%, compared with an increase in the number of 15- to 16-year-olds of just 2%.

The results published by the awarding bodies and released to candidates today cover England, Wales and Northern Ireland and relate to all entrants regardless of their age or where they took the exam.

Overall, the percentage of candidates achieving A* to C in full GCSE courses rose to 56.6% from last year's figure of 55.7%.

Last week's A-level results showed girls getting more A grades than boys for the first time, triggering a national debate about boys' so-called under-achievement.

The breakdown in GCSE results according to gender reveals some interesting trends within individual subjects.

In modern languages, for example, girls showed superior linguistic skills to their male classmates in contrast with this year's A-level results where boys' performance was ahead.

In GCSE French, 60.1% of girls got a grade C or higher, compared with 44.5% of boys. In German, the corresponding figures were 63% of girls and 49.1% of boys, while in Spanish the figures were 65.8% for girls and 51% for boys.

This year the most popular GCSE subject continued to be maths, which was taken by 673,056 candidates and accounted for around one-eighth of all the entries.

In maths, 3% of boys were awarded A*, up from 2.6% last year, while girls achieved 2.6%, up from 2.1%.

Close behind was English, with 647,436 entrants. Here, girls achieved 3.7% of A* grades in English, compared with 2% for boys, while they also picked up more As, Bs and Cs. Entries in the more traditional GCSE subjects such as biology, chemistry, physics, history and modern languages remain strong,

while art continues to be the most popular examination subject outside the national curriculum, attracting 201,296 entries. But there was a slump in entries in geography and home economics.

The subject most likely to attract the A* grade this year was again Greek. This time it was taken by only 934 candidates but nearly half of them got the top grade.

Entries for information technology were increasing significantly at all levels and types of qualification, the results show, reflecting recognition of the importance of computer skills in today's workplace.

At GCSE, for example, IT had the biggest single rise in any one subject with a 10% leap in full course entries on last year, and a corresponding 8% increase in short course entries.

The exam boards also reported that numbers of entries for GCSE short courses increased year on year by 20,698 to 275,751. They are designed to be the same standard as a full GCSE, but take half the study time.

Short course subjects with the biggest increases in entries include

5

religious education and information technology. Despite an overall decline in registrations for GNVQs, there was a sizeable increase in part one GNVQ entries, available to schools only last year.

Congratulating candidates on the results, the school standards minister, Estelle Morris, urged young people to consider staying on in further or higher education rather than quitting.

'There are plenty of opportunities to progress to higher qualifications and a more secure future,' she said, 'whether in full-time education at school or college, an apprenticeship or other vocational learning.'

Paul Sokoloff, convenor of the joint council, commented: 'The good GCSE results this year are a testimony to the hard work of students and teachers, who deserve congratulations.

'The increase in entries for GCSE, short course GCSE and part one GNVQ is good news, showing that students are taking a broader range of subjects at 16, particularly those they see as relevant to today's world. Awarding bodies will continue to innovate and to provide qualifications to meet the needs of a changing society.'

The Professional Association of Teachers welcomed the small rise in standards at GCSE and urged critics to give credit to pupils and their teachers.

But the Parents and Teachers general secretary called for a large-scale inquiry into gender differences.

'At university – where there are more male than female lecturers and few senior women academics – male students still gain more first-class degrees, while in the workplace men still dominate the top jobs in the professions, academia, politics and business,' she said.

'Even in schools, where women outnumber men, 80 per cent of secondary school headships are held by men.'

The mark of the male

A.C. Grayling has a radical answer to the furore over boys who do worse than girls in exams: just change the marking

Half-lost in the now predictable August clamour about sex differences in examination results, renewed today by publication of the GCSE results, are the old familiar clues, swirling neglected like scraps of paper in the storm around our heads.

On one page of the newspaper you read that girls are doing better than boys at A-level and GCSE, on another you read that young women get fewer firsts at Oxford than young men, on a third you read how much better all pupils perform when segregated into single-sex classes. Putting these observations together directs attention to a pivotal fact about education: that there are gender-specific differences in the way people get most benefit from it.

The single greatest change to the public examinations system in recent years has been the shift of emphasis toward course work. It is well understood that course work suits girls, and that their results are much less satisfactory if measured only by sit-down examinations at the end of the period of study. The reverse is true for boys. This explains the rising success rates for girls – and it also explains the fact that they get

fewer firsts than their male contemporaries at Oxford, where the chief measurement of attainment is still the final examination in the last weeks of the degree course.

There are some further complications to be added to this picture. Honest educators will tell you that standards are lower now than they used to be. And there is no question about it: they are far lower. Honest parents will tell you how much help they give their sons and daughters with course work, a fact that has a distorting upward effect on grades (but not on actual acquirements, since the pupils have not done all the work themselves) for both boys and girls with helpful parents. The combined effect is felt at universities, where it is no longer possible to make assumptions about what undergraduates share in the way of minimum general intellectual culture and skills.

It is also likely that the lower standards in schools, and the made-easy approaches to the subjects taught there, are dissatisfying to a significant proportion of pupils, who therefore respond with boredom and indiscipline. Pupils do not always recognise that their problem is that

they are under-stretched; instead they see school as uninteresting and unstimulating. Indiscipline is a characteristic response.

School has to compete with the much more exciting extra-mural world, with bright razzmatazz television, play-stations on computer and, for older pupils, cinema, raves, clubbing, sex and recreational drugs. If education does not seriously attract pupils' interest it is going to take a poor third place to the other multitudinous avocations of growing up.

A solution to the problem of under-stretching is streaming, that is, making sure that pupils capable of more challenging work get the chance to do it. Another aspect of the same solution is to have far smaller classes so that pupils genuinely get more individual attention. This well-worn point was allegedly refuted some years ago by publication of a report suggesting that class sizes are not a crucial factor in output success. This is true if the differences are between, say, 33 pupils per teacher and 26 pupils per teacher. But one has only to look at the achievement of private schools in getting consistently excellent grades for their pupils to see that their class sizes of 12 or 15 have to be a significant factor. That is the kind of ratio state education should be aiming at.

But the larger problem of the gender differences in achievement requires an even more radical approach, which is to recognise that boys and girls need to be assessed differently. A degree of care is needed in working out this idea. It would create all sorts of difficulties if girls were exclusively assessed by course-work methods and boys exclusively by end-of-year exams. Introducing too great a difference between the sexes in this way would be controversial because what is at stake is selection of various kinds – not least for university places.

The solution is that both sexes should be subject to both forms of assessment. A pupil's best marks should then be the ones that determine future progress. If it turned out that girls' best marks generally came from course-work assessment, and boys' generally from end-of-course exams, it would be no surprise; but it would allow for the exceptions, and would retain a basis for comparison across the sexes.

The uselessness of current comparisons between male and female exam results is not only a function of the assessment problem, but is also a result of the fact that mixed-sex classes for adolescents are not invariably a good idea, as many

teachers point out. The sexes suffer deficits in learning as a result, with different ways of compensating for them. When both boys and girls are distracted by the presence of the other sex in class, girls are more likely to make up lost ground later in homework. Girls therefore suffer marginally less from the knock-on effect of inattention in class, which is that since most subjects are learned cumulatively, lacunae in knowledge offered in earlier classes make learning in later classes more difficult.

The problem of mixed-sex classes is almost wholly one that arises in secondary education, and for the obvious adolescent reasons. A yet more radical – and actually rather good – suggestion for eliminating the problems of schooling in adolescence was offered by no less a personage than Winston Churchill.

Reflecting on his own experiences as a profoundly un-

successful schoolboy at Marlborough, he suggested that children should learn the Three Rs until puberty strikes, and should then be sent out to work until such time as their hunger and curiosity for knowledge drives them back into education – whereupon they will learn with delight, in much less time, what it now takes us years to get into adolescent heads (if ever we succeed).

His suggestion might be annexed to another, which is that education – wasted on the young, as has often enough been sagely said – should genuinely be a lifetime possibility. People should be able to move between work and education, with the support of employers and government, when need and desire arise.

Basic literacy and numeracy can be acquired in the wonderful teachable years before puberty; adolescents should be free to choose whether to stay at school or work thereafter; and the schools and universities should be open to all who, later, wish to profit from them. Coupled with a sensitivity to the way the sexes best learn, and how they best exhibit what they have learned, the education system could be a better and richer instrument as a result.

• Dr Anthony Grayling is Reader in Philosophy at Birkbeck College, London. First published in *The Guardian*, August 2000.

© *Dr Anthony Grayling*

Gender stereotypes still hamper young

By Will Woodward, Education Editor

Adolescents are still unable to shake off gender stereotypes that appear as entrenched as ever, a report by the government's Women's Unit reveals.

After a wave of anxiety about the underperformance of boys at school, the analysis, commissioned by the Cabinet Office and the Home Office, says that across adolescence both genders require different but equal attention from policy-makers.

Inside, outside and beyond school, young men and women are under continuing pressure to conform to traditional behaviour.

At school, women avoid physics and information technology and choose English, biology, history and modern languages. 'Young women

find it easier to ask for help than young men, who find it harder to admit a lack of knowledge,' the report, *Young People and Gender*, published yesterday, says.

Boys are more likely to break the law – a gap which extends after the age of 14 – or be involved in crime, alcohol abuse and illegal drugs.

Girls, who are more likely to be concerned about their body image and weight, are much more likely to start smoking. Suicide rates are higher for men and double the number of boys die at 17. Boys are less likely to visit their GP or to use other health services.

Girls are more at risk of depression, eating disorders and self-harm. Boys 'use active methods of coping, but also use much more denial than girls'.

Boys 'take greater risks and feel greater pressure' to be sexually active and find it harder to admit inexperience. But 'in spite of the notion of "girl power", young women still find it problematic to say no to sex and negotiate the use of contraception', the report says.

At work, young men are more likely to want managerial or professional jobs – 75% compared with 25% for women, who are concentrated in personal service industries with part-time jobs and lower wages. 'The need to conform to masculine stereotypes prevents young men from joining traditionally female careers.'

Although more young men are officially unemployed, a large group of young women remains outside employment, education and training

___

'At different times in the past decades public anxiety has focused on one or more of the genders, but it needs to be recognised that both young women and men may be vulnerable in different ways'

___

opportunities because of caring responsibilities.

Tessa Jowell, minister for women and employment, said: 'All young people face different pressures as they meet the challenges of the 21st century. This research underlines how important gender is to young people's behaviour, their relationships and their level of achievement.'

The research emerges from a review, the Trust for the Study of Adolescence, commissioned by the women's unit in the Cabinet Office

and the Home Office's family policy unit. The government has appointed a minister for young people, Paul Boateng.

This year, after years of outperforming boys at GCSE and most A-levels in England, Wales and Northern Ireland, girls won more A grades at A-level for the first time, provoking a spate of hand-wringing. David Blunkett, the education secretary, has promised to look at whether single-sex lessons help boys' achievement, though he is far from certain that they do.

But the report warns of the dangers of ignoring under-achieving girls. 'At different times in the past decades public anxiety has focused on one or more of the genders, but it needs to be recognised that both young women and men may be vulnerable in different ways,' it says.

'The central conclusion of this review is that it would be wrong to identify either males or females as being more in need of attention from policy-makers. Both genders have areas of their lives in which they may be at risk.'

The law on sex discrimination in education

The Sex Discrimination Act 1975 states that it is unlawful to discriminate against a person on the ground of their sex. Discrimination means less favourable treatment, and there are two kinds of discrimination:

- When a person of one sex is treated less favourably, because of his or her sex, than another person of the opposite sex, this is direct discrimination.
- When a condition or requirement is applied to both sexes, but the majority of one sex is not able to comply with it, and when the requirement cannot be justified regardless of sex and a person is disadvantaged as a result of the requirement, this is indirect discrimination.

Application of the Act at schools

In relation to schools, the Act sets out the kinds of treatment of a pupil which could be regarded as discriminatory. It states that it is unlawful to discriminate against a girl or a boy on the grounds of sex in the following ways:

- by refusing an application for their admission to the school
- by applying different terms to girls and boys in their offer to admit them to the school
- by refusing to allow girls access to any benefits, facilities or services which are open to boys, and vice versa
- by giving girls different facilities, benefits or services from boys, and vice versa

- by excluding them from school
- by subjecting them to any other detriment.

Exceptions

An exception is made for admission to single-sex schools, but the facilities available at such schools should not be inferior to those at other schools in the area. Single-sex teaching groups in co-educational schools are also lawful, provided the provision to boys and girls is equal.

For further information

Equal Opportunities Commission Scotland, St Stephens House, 279 Bath Street, Glasgow G2 4JL. Tel: 0141 248 5833. E-mail: scotland@eos.org.uk Web site: www.eoc.org.ok

Gender and education

Gender and differential achievement in education and training: a research review

Both boys and girls have improved their performance at GCSE and Standard Grade, but girls' performance has increased more rapidly than boys'. Boys are performing less well than girls in most subjects.

More than four times as many boys than girls were excluded from schools in England in 1996.

There are clear gender differences in the proportion of women and men studying particular subjects at A-level and Highers. All Sciences are dominated by men except for Biological Sciences, whereas all the Arts are dominated by women. Men and women now perform as well as each other in most subjects but in those subjects where men continue to perform better than women, the gender gap is narrowing.

Gender stereotyping is as prevalent at degree level as at other qualification levels. Men are over-represented in Engineering and Technology whereas women are over-represented in Education and the Humanities.

Further education is also heavily gender stereotyped. Young women are far more likely to study subjects allied to medicine, the social sciences or creative arts whereas young men are more likely to study mathematical

**EQUAL
OPPORTUNITIES
COMMISSION**

sciences, agriculture, engineering or technology. Youth training and Modern Apprenticeships also display gender stereotyping of occupation.

Similar percentages of young men and women now study for GNVQ/GSVQs but men are more likely than women to be studying for NVQ/SVQ and non-NVQ/SVQ vocational qualifications. Women are more likely than men to study A-levels and Highers through further education.

Introduction
The Equal Opportunities Commission (EOC) views education as pivotal in the process of achieving equality of opportunity between men and women. The choices made and standards achieved in education and training remain influential for the whole of people's working and social lives.

The Commission has recently conducted an in-house research review to look at the available literature on achievement in education and training. Data are rarely available for Great Britain overall as the Scottish secondary system differs from that in England and Wales. Not only is the curriculum different, but a separate system of examinations and qualifications is followed. Thus, research relevant to this review generally focuses on the education and qualification system in England and Wales or that in Scotland, as identified in the text. The final section is devoted to the situation in Scotland.

It is hoped that the findings from the review will broaden the current debate surrounding achievement to consider not only that, but also the different access, choices, and destinations of young women and men.

Background
The EOC has been concerned about the differential achievement of girls and boys in education and training since it was set up over 20 years ago. On average, girls now out-perform boys at GCSE/SCE Standard Grade and there is widespread concern about boys' achievement at this level.

The situation with regard to A-level and Highers examination performance, degree attainment and vocational training and qualifications is more complex. At all qualification levels, gender stereotyping of subjects is prevalent wherever choice is allowed, with implications for future employment possibilities.

Different groups of students have always achieved better or worse examination results than others. When the Sex Discrimination Act was introduced in 1975 concern rested firmly with girls' disadvantage. Now, through an emphasis on standards and quantifiable levels of achievement, concern is focused on the performance of boys and their 'underachievement'.

The term 'underachievement' can lead to confusion. It contains no indication of what achievement is measured against. Although there are differences between boys and girls in terms of achievement, other factors are also of importance. Every year, a number of boys *and* girls leave school at the age of 16 without any qualifications, whereas others, of both sexes, achieve five or more GCSEs or Standard Grade at the highest grade.

A research review was needed to clarify some of the issues which concern the EOC, and to reflect the available literature on achievement in relation to gender. The aim was to determine what is meant by differential achievement, and to identify who, how and why certain groups are underachieving relative to others in the education and training system.

The methodology involved a traditional desk review of the available literature accessing a number of sources, attendance at seminars and the use of the EOC Research Database to identify the names of individual researchers who have an interest in education and training.

Key findings of the review
Compulsory schooling
Girls are noticeably outperforming boys across all areas at the age of seven, and in English at the ages of eleven and fourteen. More boys than girls tend to score at the extremes, either very high or very low.

Despite the National Curriculum, where choice is allowed at GCSE certain subjects continue to show a distinct gender bias. The majority of Science subjects are dominated by boys, the majority of Arts subjects by girls, whereas the Social Sciences are more mixed.

Girls are clearly outperforming boys in most subjects at GCSE and Standard Grade. Both boys and girls have benefited from more varied styles of teaching and assessment, and have improved their performance at GCSE level and equivalent, but girls' performance has increased more rapidly than that of boys.

Choice has been reintroduced to compulsory schooling through the Part One GNVQs in England and Wales. With clearly gender-stereotyped subject areas like health and social care, manufacturing and engineering, there are concerns that young people may be encouraged to make occupational choices far too early, thereby reducing their future employment possibilities.

Care needs to be taken that any measures which seek to improve the performance of one group of pupils are not at the expense of other pupils. For example, boys are known to benefit from more structured and rule-bound lessons than girls, who prefer more discussion-led and collaborative lessons.

More than four times as many boys than girls were excluded from schools in England in 1996. Black pupils were far more likely to be excluded than White or Asian pupils, possibly due to the different interpretations placed on their behaviour by teaching staff.

Gender is not the only factor influencing achievement in school. Ethnicity and social class are also significant, but unfortunately, most available data do not take more than one variable into account, often due to small sample sizes. The situation with regard to ethnicity is particularly complex.

The GCSE league table in England is headed primarily by single-sex schools, and those that are independent or public. These schools are highly selective: ability and social class are more important factors than the single-sex nature of the schools.

A-levels, Highers and Higher Education
There are clear gender differences in the proportions of men and women studying particular subjects at A-level and in Highers. All Sciences except for Biological Science are dominated by men, whereas all the Arts are dominated by women. As with GCSE, Social Sciences show a mixed gender distribution.

Men and women now perform as well as each other in most subjects at A-level and Highers. In those subjects where men continue to perform better than women, the gender gap is narrowing.

At A-level, a cross-over in patterns of performance is apparent compared with results at GCSE, whereby more men than women achieve higher level grades in certain subjects.

Social background is significantly related to performance at A-level and Highers, with children from professional, associate professional, managerial and technical occupations gaining a higher average score than children from other backgrounds.

In recent years, higher education has experienced an enormous expansion. There are now very similar numbers of men and women in higher education, but the numbers of women have grown far more rapidly than those of men. From constituting one-third of undergraduates in 1975, women now make up slightly more than one-half.

Men and women participate in different types of post graduate study. Men are more likely than women to be studying for a higher degree through research or on a taught course, but are less likely to be taking some 'other' form of taught course. Twice as many women than men study for a post graduate teaching qualification.

Gender stereotyping is as prevalent at degree level as in other qualification levels. Men are over-represented in Engineering and Technology whereas women are over-represented in Education and the Humanities.

In British universities overall, women achieve proportionately more good degrees than men. Men achieve slightly more first-class degrees than women. A far greater proportion of women achieve an upper second degree. The situation differs in individual institutions, and on average, men at 'Oxbridge' achieve better degrees than women.

Men and women interviewed during their degree courses have different expectations after graduation. Women are more cautious and tend to underestimate their skills development. They are more likely to take temporary or part-time work than men, and have less considered career plans.

Men with Science, Engineering and Technology degrees are more likely than women to enter management or a professional occupation allied to their degree. Women are more likely than men to enter teaching.

Further education and vocational training

Young men are more likely to study mathematical sciences, agriculture or engineering and technology and young women are more likely to study subjects allied to medicine, the social sciences or the creative arts. Hairdressing, secretarial studies and health and social care are known as the three 'women's areas' in further education.

Women are more likely than men to study A-levels and Highers through further education. Similar percentages of young women and men now study for GNVQs, but a greater percentage of men than women study for NVQs and other, traditional vocational qualifications.

Similar proportions of men and women now participate in Youth Training, complete their training, gain a qualification and find a job. Young women are more likely than men to be working towards a lower level qualification, to be paid an allowance rather than a wage and to be on YT because they could not find a job or join a college course of their choice.

Pupils achieving GCSE grades A-C*: by selected subject and gender

- Although girls are outperforming boys in public examinations there remain gender differences in the subjects studied.
- The traditional gender divide is narrowing and girls are doing better in traditionally 'male' subjects.
- In 1988/89 a third of girls achieved a GCSE grade A* to C in a science subject and this proportion rose to 46 per cent in 1995/96.
- In 1988 nearly two out of ten boys achieved a GCSE grade A* to C in a foreign language and this proportion rose to nearly three out of ten in 1995/96.

Percentage	Males			Females		
	1988/89	1992/93	1995/96	1988/89	1992/93	1995/96
English	38	44	43	53	61	61
Any science	35	41	45	33	41	46
Mathematics	36	39	42	32	40	43
Any modern language	19	24	28	30	37	43
French	17	20	20	27	31	32
History	16	17	17	18	22	22
Geography	21	22	24	18	20	23

Source: Department for Education and Employment; National Assembly for Wales; Scottish Executive

The costs of training to employers vary depending on the type of industry. Substantially more is spent on trainees in sectors which have a tradition of apprenticeships like construction and engineering where the trainees are mainly young men, than on trainees in the hotel and catering industry or local authorities where there is more even gender balance.

Apprenticeships have always been gender segregated, and those in the Modern Apprenticeship scheme

---

Some children in the compulsory schooling sector, mainly boys, are alienated from education and facing 'social exclusion'

---

are no exception. Young people were encouraged into areas which already operated an apprenticeship scheme and as a result, traditional gender stereotyping has persisted. Many sectors are strongly gender biased including the two most popular sectors, engineering manufacturing and business administration.

Any attempt to examine vocational training and qualifications is hampered by the lack of accurate data disaggregated by gender. Many official analyses still do not consider gender as a variable.

Conclusions

Some children in the compulsory schooling sector, mainly boys, are alienated from education and facing 'social exclusion'. In addition, the subject choices of both boys and girls impact upon their future employment possibilities.

Boys' subject choice excludes them from clerical and caring

occupations where many of the new job opportunities exist. And although girls and young women are performing well in examinations at all levels, their subject choice automatically excludes them from scientific and technological professions which require specialisation at an early age.

Certain measures have been shown to improve boys' concentration and performance in individual schools. A 'good practice guide' for practitioners showing what can work would prove invaluable. It is important that any measures should be monitored and evaluated to ensure that all pupils have the opportunity to benefit from their implementation. In addition, there is a need to place the school experience in a wider societal context to address attitudes towards the role of parents and family, education, employment, unemployment and individual expectations.

One of the most important omissions is the lack of good quality, accurate data on the qualifications, performance and employment experience of young people disaggregated, at the very least, by gender and preferably also by ethnicity and social class.

Scotland

At the age of 14, pupils in Scotland choose Standard Grade subjects from eight curricular modes. Gender stereotyping of choice remains, and is likely to be greater for working-class than for middle-class pupils.

Although the average examination performance of boys and girls has increased at Standard Grade, girls have progressed more rapidly than boys. Girls are less likely than boys to leave school with no educational qualification.

Traditionally girls have done well in English and they continue to achieve better results than boys in this subject at Standard Grade. Despite a steady increase in the numbers of boys taking French and German, girls' performance improved relative to boys in Modern Foreign Languages during the 1990s. Similar numbers of girls and boys take Mathematics and achieve comparable results.

The Standard Grade examina-

tion enables performance in different elements of a subject to be analysed. Girls tend to do well on internally assessed elements whereas boys' grades are more variable than girls, for example, in problem solving in Science.

The number of school exclusions appears to be very low in Scotland compared with England and Wales. However, this is partly due to the way in which 'exclusion' is defined and the data are collected in Scotland. Gender disaggregated data on the number of exclusions are not collected.

A greater proportion of young women compared with young men stay on in post-compulsory education. Continuing participation is closely linked with educational attainment, gender and social class.

The high attaining group at Standard Grade has the highest participation in S5, S6 and HE; the middle attaining group is the most likely to enter FE; and the low attaining group tend to enter Youth Training. Men are more likely than women to enter some form of training.

Boys' subject choice excludes them from clerical and caring occupations where many of the new job opportunities exist

---

Overall, a greater percentage of girls than boys leave school with at least one Higher Grade. Until the mid 1980s, similar percentages of girls and boys left school with five or more Highers but by the mid 1990s, a five per cent gap had emerged in favour of girls. This is a considerable improvement in girls' performance relative to that of boys. Overall, however, there is little difference in the average scores of young women and men who take and achieve examinations at Higher Grade, unlike the more apparent differences at Standard Grade.

The Scottish School Leavers Survey (SSLS) illustrates interesting differences between young women and men and the type of training scheme or job which they enter. Gender stereotyping is clearly apparent. At the time of the last SSLS for which data are currently available (1995), one in three women were in clerical and secretarial jobs/training schemes whereas more than two out of five men were in craft and related jobs/training schemes.

A greater percentage of men than women develop further qualifications through on and off the job training or through a recognised apprenticeship. The Modern Apprenticeship scheme in Scotland has been less influential due in part to the more established nature of Skillseekers. Even so, training opportunities are found mainly in traditionally male dominated sectors.

© *Equal Opportunities Commission (EOC)*

Battle of sexes set for truce

Information from The Future Foundation

From the struggle for suffrage, to burning bras and smashing through the glass ceiling, the battle of the sexes has waged for decades, but a truce looks set to be declared in 2015.

According to research by Abbey National, equality between men and full-time working women in the home will take place in 15 years' time, when males and full-time working females will be doing the same number of hours of cooking and cleaning.

And the good news for women who aren't prepared to wait more than a decade for their partners to pick up a tea towel is that two-thirds of modern men already do far more around the home than their fathers did. Similar numbers of women claim to do much less housework than their mothers, with careers and families taking preference over the dusting and ironing.

The bank identified the significant milestone after working with sociologists at think tank The Future Foundation, and is just one of the findings highlighted in its *Complicated Lives* Report. The report is designed to help Abbey National understand life's complications and develop flexible products that suit customers' increasingly hectic lifestyles.

The research confirms there has been a seismic shift in the gender gap. Lorna Waddell of Abbey National says: 'The blurring of the roles of the sexes is largely attributable to women's increased economic activity. In 1951, for example, only one in four married women went out to work. Today that figure is more than 70 per cent. This has clearly had an effect on men, who are taking more responsibility for household chores and parenting.'

The Abbey National study also highlights how men's overall share of housework has been boosted by the increasing numbers of single-person households, most of which are men. Single men under the age of 65 made up just four per cent of all households in 1978 – today, they account for more than eight per cent. According to the futurologists, all of these trends are set to continue. More women will enter the workforce, due to the rise of employment in the service sector, and as employers increasingly offer flexible and shorter hours and more childcare provision. In fact, experts predict that there will be more female than male employees in the workplace by the end of 2001.

Michael Willmott, co-founder of The Future Foundation, said: 'It no longer makes sense to rely on traditional roles when dividing up tasks in the home. Instead, new roles must be negotiated by every couple depending on their individual circumstances. In the future, the important thing will be who has the time – or the inclination – to do housework, and not whether they are a man or woman.'

• The above findings are taken from a report – *Complicated Lives* – commissioned by Abbey National through The Future Foundation. The report pulls together new quantitative and qualitative research with extensive analysis of over 100 different social trends. In addition, NOP conducted more than 950 interviews with adults aged 18 and above between 28 January and 30 January 2000. The NOP sample was designed to be representative of adults in Great Britain. These findings were further explored in national focus groups where researchers quizzed three generations of families. Covering six key areas of modern life – and its complications – the report looks at parenting, jobs, consumerism and possessions, worries and money.

© *The Future Foundation*

Women in the UK

The shape of things to come

The last 25 years have brought a massive transformation in women's lives in the UK. To help them manage this change, women want their voices to be heard and their life choices to be valued. This was the unmistakable message from the Women's National Commission (WNC) today. For their latest report, *Future Female – A 21st Century Gender Perspective*, the WNC, in partnership with The Future Foundation, quizzed women from all over the country on their hopes and fears for the future. Groups ranging from working women to non-working women, ethnic minority women, older women and younger women, were presented with the findings of an exhaustive review of statistics on the lives of women today, and predictions for tomorrow. They were asked what mattered most to them at the start of a new century.

The report identifies the degree to which women's lives have already changed, and highlights the big issues going forward. Speaking from the Women's National Commission's Cabinet Office base, the WNC's Chair, Baroness Christine Crawley, said, 'Women's lives have changed so much. New family structures and economic change have reshaped women's roles and possibilities. Yet so many old burdens still fall on women's shoulders. This report is a fascinating inventory of facts and figures – as well as opinions – that really matter. We will all spend less of our lives in primary caring roles, as women now have just 1.7 babies on average – a significant decrease on the oft-quoted 2.4 children; lone parents head a quarter of families with children; and in spite of the hugely increasing numbers of women in paid work, 1.2 million women care for an elderly parent. Living in an ageing society is going to be one of the biggest challenges for women going forward – not just as older women themselves but as the main carers for the elderly. We are only just beginning to understand the scale of the burden this will present.'

Baroness Crawley commented, 'Even with such diversity in women's lives, it's fascinating to see how much agreement there is about what really matters. Women everywhere have been telling us very forcefully that they want the often unpaid contribution that they make to the community to be properly recognised. They want employers to support them as they try to balance their home lives with their work lives. They want policy makers to recognise that families now take very many different forms. And they want to see more women involved in making the decisions and policies that affect all our lives.'

'Increasing levels of education, growing income and savings and access to technology, all spell more opportunity for women to take control of their own lives and financial futures', notes Melanie Howard of The Future Foundation, co-author of the report, 'but the lack of effective female representation in management and politics and the larger unpaid caring and domestic burden that women bear in comparison with men means that there is a long way to go before equality of opportunity is a reality for all women in the 21st century.'

• *Future Female – A 21st Century Gender Perspective* is a comprehensive collation of facts and opinion, representing the views of some of the millions of members of the Women's National Commission.

Notes

1. The WNC is an independent advisory body to Government set up by Harold Wilson in 1969. Its remit is to ensure that the informed opinion of women is given its due weight in the deliberations of government and in public debate on matters of public interest, including in particular those which may be considered as of special interest to women.

2. The Future Foundation is a commercial think-tank founded in 1996. It aims to bring a better understanding of the impact of social trends on business planning for the future; and, where possible, to promote increased corporate social responsibility through greater awareness. They can be contacted on 020 7250 3343.

3. Further information about the WNC can be found on its website: www.thewnc.org.uk.

Mind the pay gap
The cost of being a woman

SKILLS LEVEL	GENDER GAP – the cost of being female	MOTHER GAP – the impact on a woman's lifetime earnings of having two children	PARENT GAP – the difference in earnings between a mother of two and a father of two
Low skilled (no qualifications)	£197,000	£285,000	£482,000
Mid skilled (qualifications to GCSE level)	£241,000	£140,000	£381,000
High skilled (graduate)	£143,000	£19,000	£161,000

Source: Women's Incomes Over the Lifetime, February 2000

Background situation

Information from the United Kingdom Men's Movement

We have a historical legacy of unequal treatment in society of men and women. However due to various factors and chivalry, in its wider sense, it has often been men who were treated less equally. For instance the dramatic difference in state pension provisions, and the lack of health care programmes specific to men.

But we have also seen many measures in the last 30 years to promote women's roles in society, but unfortunately also to deliberately reduce that of men beyond what most people would consider reasonable. Most of these have been driven by a vociferous minority of radical feminist groups. The establishment of the Equal Opportunities Commission in 1975 has been one major step. Its activities are not however about equality, but about promoting women's rights, and reducing men's.

Parliament and the Government appear not to see the wider picture, but continue to develop anti-male policies and legislation. As examples, we have recently seen the introduction of a Minister for Women, but not one for men, as well as steps to ensure that all new legislation is woman-friendly. The Government statements on such matters appear at first to be innocuous, but consider for a moment the implications of having a Minister for Women and what 'woman-friendly' means in practice.

Discrimination against men is outlined in our publication of that name. The major areas of concern are :
- state pension entitlement
- health care provision for men
- the divorce racket and social policies which reduce men's rights in the family
- lack of equal educational and training provisions to men
- less than fair treatment in civil and criminal law
- women-only facilities

- the imbalance of men's groups compared with women's
- the general denigration of men, and lack of representation of men's issues in the media
- the lack of representation of men's issues in Parliament and the Government.

It has been in response to this situation that men's groups have been created since the 1970s. Of the issues listed above, it is matrimonial and family law, and social policies about the family, which have had the hardest effects on men. It has been no surprise that groups addressing these issues first arose.

In 1989 Dads after Divorce was founded by four men, each of whom had been the victim of engineered divorce petitions alleging their unreasonable behaviour. DADs was involved in the establishment of the Cheltenham Group, and of the UKMM. DADs was formed largely as a response to the United Kingdom divorce racket.

The Child Support Act was passed in 1990. The concealed agenda behind the Act was to force non-liable persons to pay the social security benefits of legal strangers. Fathers completely accept that children need to be supported financially and to be cared for by both parents.

However fathers object to being financially crippled in supporting an ex-spouse who divorced them and took away their children that they are hardly ever allowed to see. It is this matter relating to the children's issues that is the most contentious area of divorce.

In 1996 the Family Law Act received its third reading. This bill basically established in law the concept of No-Fault Divorce, i.e. that divorce should take place on the basis of unilateral unsubstantiated demand.

The United Kingdom Men's Movement was founded in July 1994 to rally all the forces in the UK which are now beginning to react against uncontrolled feminism and its disastrous social consequences. DADs has now amalgamated with the UKMM.

• The above information is from the United Kingdom Men's Movement's web site which can be found at www.ukmm.org.uk
© *The United Kingdom Men's Movement*

Changing gender relationships

The situation at European level

All societies in the Member States of the European Union are organised around an implicit social contract. For almost 2000 years the economy was organised around the fact that women stay at home, take care of the children and do the domestic work, men being the 'breadwinner'. In that way, men were able to work outside the home in part because women were doing all the other tasks (taking care of the children, of the home, of their clothes . . .).

In the last decades this social contract has been changed little by little by the fight for women's rights and the evolution of society: the increasing participation of women in the labour market, the women's right to vote, the existence of contraception, and therefore the possibility for women to control the number of children they have. Women didn't want any more to be relegated to the private sphere. The question is, has this evolution of women's role been followed by new gender relationships based on equality between the partners? Have men's roles in society and in the house changed proportionally?

There is a general thought among young people in the 90s that there is no need to fight for gender equality in society any more, because the new gender relationship already exists and is fully based upon equality between partners.

However, the opinion among young people themselves brings a different point of view: most young people think that women have equal career opportunities in the 90s (62%). But if a young woman is aspiring to become a pilot, vicar or bus driver, 43%, 40% and 38% of the young people would consider a man better suited for these jobs.

If gender relationships have truly changed in the last 30 years, stereotypes and the classical division of tasks are still well alive, even for young couples.

One of the major difficulties young women still encounter in Europe today is to reconcile their professional with their family life, due to the persisting unequal distribution of tasks in society and at home. Some data may illustrate the actual situation in most European Union Member States:

- Women's total fertility rate declined by 45% from 1960 to

One of the major difficulties young women still encounter in Europe today is to reconcile their professional life with their family life

---

1995, from 2.59 to 1.43 children per woman in the EU. There are still differences among the Member States of the European Union, ranging from 1.87 in Ireland to 1.18 in Spain.

- Responsibility for the care of dependent persons still constitutes an obstacle to the full participation and advancement of women in the labour market. There is a gender imbalance in the entire approach to caring, with the persistence of the assumption that care is the responsibility of women.

- The vast majority of single parents are women (around 9 out of 10 single parents are women). This is directly linked with the increase of the proportion of divorced, separated and never married lone parents in the Member States of the EU. This simple fact clearly illustrates that,

---

Economic activity status of women[1]

By marital status and age of youngest dependent child, spring 1999

- The growth in women working since 1945 has been greatest among married women. So by 1999, three-quarters of married or cohabiting women of working age were economically active.

- Among women with dependent children those with a partner are more likely to be economically active than those without, especially when their children are young.

- In 1999, six in ten married or cohabiting women with a child under 5 worked compared with three out of ten lone mothers.

Percentage	Age of youngest dependent child				No dependent children	All
Married/cohabiting	Under 5	5-10	11-15	16-18[2]		
Working full time	21	25	37	41	50	38
Working part time	38	50	42	38	25	34
Unemployed[3]	3	3	2	–	2	2
Economically inactive	38	22	19	20	23	25
All (= 100%)(millions)	2.3	1.7	1.2	0.5	5.2	10.9

1 All women aged 16 to 59.
2 Those in full-time education.
3 Based on the ILO definition.

Source: Labour Force Survey, Office for National Statistics

in spite of all the social changes that have taken place in recent years and in spite of changing expectations about the roles of men and women, it is still women who are responsible for bringing up children. Lone-parent families represent around 10% of households in Europe.

- 83% of part-time workers in the European Union are women. Part-time work is often considered as a means to reconcile work and family life. For some women it is not an option, it is the only thing they can do due to the lack of affordable care facilities and the lack of sharing commitment from the male partner.
- The use of parental leave by men is still very low: 7 men for 100 women in Denmark in 1995, 1 man for 100 women in France in 1992, 2 men for 100 women in Germany in 1995. This is also linked to the fact that women are usually in lower paid jobs or are less paid for the same job, it is therefore they who have to quit their jobs, because the salary loss for the family is lesser.

(The differences in the percentage of children attending public funded childcare facilities differ enormously from one Member State to other. In Denmark it is about 48% of the children aged 0-3 meanwhile in Spain, Ireland or UK it is about 2% of the children of the same age. This is clearly showing the lack of care services in some countries, which makes it difficult to work and have children.)

- Figures also show that women in high decision-making positions have fewer children: 41.9% of women in management positions don't have any children (while the majority of men in the same positions do have children in majority) and 90.8% cannot afford a career break.
- There is a percentage of the female working population in the European Union, which is classified as 'assisting spouses' (in the agriculture or in small businesses). Those are spouses who are neither associates nor do they receive any salary from the business, but who participate in the activity of the self-employed by fulfilling tasks which are either identical or complementary to those of the official head of the business, usually the husband. They do not have pension rights when they retire; nor do they have rights to social protection.

When talking of marginalised groups of women and changing gender relationships the problems mentioned above are intensified:

Migrant and ethnic minority women face in many cases aggravated social stereotypes. Their attempts to change traditional discriminatory behaviours could be misunderstood as an attack on their cultural or religious patterns. Migrant and ethnic minority women are often excluded from the social services provided by States, because of their illegal status in the country or their lack of information, preventing them from access to childcare, unemployment benefits, etc.

Many ethnic minority women enter the Member States of the EU with 'derived rights', that is: their right to residence is linked to their husband's status, which means that in the event of separation, divorce or death of the husband, they may face deportation. The probationary period before individual rights are granted lasts between one and four years, depending on the Member State in question. The lack of legal status further reinforces stereotypical images of ethnic minority women as mere appendages to men, dependent on men in every way.

Concerning another marginalised group, lesbian women suffer discrimination because they do not fit into the traditional family patterns. Their right not to form a family or to define one's own family is not recognised. This discrimination sometimes prevents them from accessing social security, housing, inheritage rights, taxes benefits, immigration law application, etc.

What can be done?

- Create a new gender contract, that means new definition on the gender roles in society, taking into account all issues related to the life cycle of both women and men and not solely the needs of one or the other. This concept might contribute to the possibility of the full participation of women in decision-making, both quantitatively as well as qualitatively, thus giving voice and opportunity to integrate women's talents and expertise into the policy process.
- Support and establish a number of different measures to facilitate the combination of work and caring responsibilities, including time-related provisions as leave arrangements to be equally shared by women and men, reduced working hours. Social security systems should also recognise the valuable contribution of caring to society. Family-friendly working policies are also essential, in particular paid parental leave.
- Societies have to recognise that men have been able to work full time and occupy high decision-making positions because women were taking care of everything else (i.e. children, homework, buying their clothes, cooking for their houses and colleagues, etc.).
- Affordable, sufficient and good quality care for children and the elderly is a responsibility of the society and should be fully taken on board by governments.
- Awareness raising campaigns to change mentalities, fight stereotypes and allow women a free choice in their role in society (option to have a family or not, work or being at home, etc.).
- Make visible the 'invisible' work of women at home, through the economic recognition of the work developed by women at home with all its consequences (economic benefits, pension rights, insurance, etc.).
- Measures aimed at preventing teenage pregnancy.
- Sexual education in freedom at schools.

• The above information is from the European Women's Lobby's web site which can be found at www.womenlobby.org

© European Women's Lobby (EWL)

Waddaya mean, the war's over?

In the public arena, the battle between the sexes appears to rage on . . . but in the privacy of our own homes, are we edging towards a ceasefire? Dave Hill reports on new research that suggests just that.

What is brought to mind by the words 'gender debate'? Reflections on the striving of the sexes to make sweet music together, seated side by side on the same piano stool? Probably not. More likely the term signals discord and dismay. It evokes terrifying 'findings' that having a job and a family – 'having it all' – is making mothers and their children miserable. Or maybe it makes you think of frightening statistics showing that as women rise in the professions, the boardroom or the classroom, men and boys are sinking in despair.

If so, who could blame you? Social commentators add to the impression that there can be no brave new settlement between the sexes, only a 'sex war', portrayed as being fought out between all men on one side and all women on the other. Even when the sexes are identified as having some interest in common, the currency of mutual antagonism rules. A TV ad designed to sell the same car to male and female drivers does so by means of clashing archetypes – a caricature bloke talking down to womankind, a cartoon coquette returning the favour.

Do such depictions reflect reality? And are they helpful to the majority of people as they try to adjust to changing times? Emphatically not, according to a report out today. Though optimistically entitled *The Sexual Renaissance*, it exposes a serious dislocation between public debate about gender and citizens' real concerns over the significance of their sex and its influence on their lives.

Drawing on in-depth interviews with focus groups of 'opinion leaders' from marketing and advertising, the media and politics, and 50 members of the public – 25 women, 25 men – the report's author, Sue Tibballs, concludes that the debate's 'ambivalence and inertia' leaves unaddressed the challenges faced by men and women as old sex-based identities erode.

Furthermore, she finds it promotes 'regressive trends that put pressure on individuals to remain within traditional roles, while introducing a tone of moral censure and personal blame that exacerbates the real problems women and men already endure'. Result? Confusion, worry and guilt.

Tibballs, who also conceived and managed the project, is intriguingly qualified for her task. A freelance communications strategist who specialises in 'gender issues and corporate responsibility', she is acquainted with both the academy of gender and the world of commerce.

She began her career as an activist with the Women's Environmental Network and later worked as a government consultant in the run-up to the Fourth United Nations World Conference on Women, held in Beijing in 1995. Until a year ago, she was women's affairs campaigner at the Body Shop, where she ran the company's body-image promotion of Ruby, the Rubenesque Doll; prior to that she was executive director of the Women's Communication Centre, a 'virtual think-tank' and publisher of *The Sexual Renaissance*.

Tibballs began the project considering the question of whether a gender debate was still necessary. She has concluded that it most definitely is, but that the terms on which it is conducted need to move on sharply. The evidence of her survey, she argues, demands a new and more productive 'gender paradigm' to replace those that have become outdated or rendered destructive by unruly propaganda.

It must be one that 'recognises today's more complex relationship between gender and equality' and 'understands that both women and men can experience inequality, and also that women's and men's interests are often entwined'.

Such a paradigm would entail a shift away from a concern with 'formal democratic equality' towards one with 'substantive social equality'. In other words, less of a pre-occupation with comparing the respective rights and statuses of the sexes, and more close-up inquiry into the actual lives of men and women in a society in which broad generalisations about both do less justice than ever to social realities.

The 'substantive' model of debate, Tibballs believes, has the flexibility to accommodate diversity among the sexes as well as growing areas of common ground, such as the desire in many couples for both partners to have careers and contribute equally to bringing up children.

At the same time, it would acknowledge people's clear recognition that their sex still makes a difference, both in the way they feel about themselves and the way others feel about them – often to their disadvantage.

Simply put, a gender debate reconfigured on such terms would help us to get to grips with our contradictions and confusions – and as Tibballs' research shows, there is no shortage of those. For every theme to emerge showing awareness of disparities between the sexes, there was another insisting not too much should be made of them – certainly nothing political.

It came out strongly that gender issues are overwhelmingly and disparagingly associated with feminism . . . and feminism with sectarian man-haters. Less discouragingly, there was resistance to the identification of particular issues exclusively with one sex or the other. As one female 'opinion leader' remarked: 'Families, poverty, equality, opportunity are things that touch men as well as women.'

Tibballs sees such perceptions as characterising 'an age of ambivalence' wherein the belief that men and women are different – in some ways, valuably so – co-exists with the conviction that they should be treated as the same. At the same time, the feeling prevails that the social constraints imposed by our sex are not a proper object of political action (there were notably mixed views about the existence of a minister for women).

This ambivalence was common to both 'opinion leaders' and the public, but perhaps the most worrying finding is how pronounced it was among the former. These often showed themselves chronically inhibited by their own prejudices – notably about feminism – and by an inability to think past categories and labels they disliked.

Predictably, the male opinion leaders were most likely to dismiss gender issues as unimportant or passé yet all seemed paralysed by the very stereotypes in which their own industries habitually trade and have, of course, done a great deal to create.

Asked about this variance, Tibballs says she noted with great interest that 'the general public groups were more progressive than the "opinion formers" in the sense that they were much more aware of the need for support to combine roles for the simple reason that circumstances have forced them to renegotiate those roles'.

When asked to talk about the nuts and bolts of their daily existence, these men and women showed themselves thoroughly receptive to the idea of a 'gender debate', even though they were put off by the actual expression. It seemed, in fact, that they were debating gender among themselves the whole time.

Tibballs believes if these private conversations were reflected on more public platforms – in the communications industries and in politics – it would greatly benefit the majority of women and men who have already been won over to the principle of equality and are now trying to figure out how to enjoy its benefits. The burning question seems to be: when will the leaders of opinion in this country catch up with the rest of us?

Why the future belongs to women

Women in their 30s and 40s will be the most powerful force in society in only 20 years, with more spending power and influence than any other group, according to a survey.

The future is female as women enjoy greater opportunities, better resources, increased prospects and more freedom of choice, says *Cosmopolitan* magazine. Baroness Jay, Minister for Women, said: 'The 21st century will be one in which women's potential comes fully alive.

'Our lives have changed enormously over the past 100 years and we share women's desire for more choice and greater control in the new millennium.

'I believe the next millennium will be the one for women. We are going to see them not only making progress, but making great achievements in all aspects of their lives.'

Girls already outperform their male peers at GCSE and A-level, more are enrolling at university, and once there, 53 per cent receive firsts and seconds compared to 47 per cent of men.

On average, women earn 80 per cent of male earnings, but for women in their 20s the pay gap shrinks by half and will soon vanish altogether. The number of women in senior management has doubled since the early 1990s and while the average male manager is 43 and has been with his company for 17 years, his female counterpart is 37 and has been with the company only 11 years.

Female managers' salaries are also rising at 7.7 per cent compared with 6.8 per cent for men.

A man's place in the home

Fathers and families in the UK

The part that fathers play in their children's upbringing is receiving unprecedented scrutiny from policy makers. Yet there is widespread confusion and disagreement over the contribution men make to contemporary family life. Charlie Lewis, Professor of Psychology at the University of Lancaster, draws on findings from recent research to summarise what is known about fathers and fatherhood in Britain.

The policy focus on fathers

Fathers have become central figures on the policy agenda, but often in the negative context of absence from their children's lives at crucial times.

- Despite the image of the absentee father and historically high levels of divorce, 7 out of 10 families consist of dependent children living with both their birth parents.
- Seventy per cent of non-resident fathers have contact with their children.
- Many men feel they are under pressure both to earn the major income for their families and to care for their children. British fathers:
  – work the longest hours in the Europe Union (an average 48 hours a week for those with children under 11);
  – continue to earn an average two-thirds of family incomes.
- Although mothers still carry the major share of household and childcare responsibilities, parents in dual-earner households commonly report that childcare is equally shared.
- In a substantial minority of households with dependent children, fathers are the main carers while mothers are out at work.
- Men who work long hours and share the childcare responsibilities with their partners are more likely than others to report feeling stressed and dissatisfied with their lives.

- Despite the increasingly 'hands-on' reality of fathering for many men, cultural stereotypes of fathers as 'providers' and 'breadwinners' continue to exert a strong influence over men, women and children's attitudes to parenthood.

Policy issues

Policy debates about fatherhood continue to be dominated by an 'economic' view of fathering. There is little serious discussion about what policy makers and service providers can actually do to support men's parenting:

- Legal definitions of fathering and fatherhood stress the importance of biological links between men and children.
- The debate about 'absentee fathers' has focused on men's economic responsibilities towards their children, to the neglect of father-child relationships.
- Almost four out of ten babies each year are born into cohabiting relationships, yet few fathers obtain Parental Responsibility Agreements or Orders. This means they lack any legal right to be involved in important decisions about their children's upbringing.

- Current Government initiatives such as Sure Start, the National Childcare Strategy and the National Family and Parenting Institute offer an opportunity to raise the profile of fathers within family support services.
- There are major cultural and social obstacles that will need to be overcome before fathers can be fully included in mainstream family services that have traditionally targeted and been used by mothers.
- Attempts in Britain to limit the working week have the potential to influence the quantity of father-child contact and the quality of family relationships. It is too early to know what effect they will produce.

Introduction

The contribution made by fathers to their children's welfare and development has received increasing recognition in recent years from policy makers. As the Government's 1998 consultation paper *Supporting Families* puts it: 'Fathers have a crucial role to play in their children's upbringing'. But fathering and fatherhood have also come under unprecedented scrutiny. The stereotypical division of parental roles that emerged during the last century between bread-winning, disciplinarian fathers, and mothers as non-earning housekeepers and carers, does not match the reality for most contemporary families. Yet there is continuing confusion over the part men actually play in today's families, and a lack of consensus about their potential role in child-rearing. Modern fathers are occasionally portrayed as 'new' or even 'super' dads, sharing childcare and home-care tasks with their partners while successfully balancing their family responsibilities with paid work. But more often, the media spotlight shines on men as 'deadbeat' dads – no more able to parent and support their children than they are to keep a steady job. Away from these extremes, recent research has sought to create a clearer picture of contemporary fatherhood and of the factors that promote or prevent active fathering. This article draws together findings from 21 recent research projects relevant to fathers, most of them supported by the Joseph Rowntree Foundation.

Fathers and children

The rapid pace of family change in the past 30 years should not obscure the fact that most families (around seven out of ten) still consist of children living with both biological parents. Around 10 per cent are children living with one biological parent and a step-parent. More than eight in ten fathers of dependent children in the 1992 British Household Panel Study were found to be living with all their own, biological children – and more than seven in ten were doing so within their first family.

Fathers, on average, earn two-thirds of family incomes. Research also suggests that mothers in two-parent households still typically carry the major share of routine household responsibilities and of caring for children and other dependants. Men, whether they are teenagers or the fathers of teenage children, tend to explain this lesser contribution at home in terms of a man's prerogative to provide for his family. Other parenting activities are viewed as

additions to that central task. But an unequal share of domestic responsibilities does not mean that providing an income for their children is all that fathers do.

Although fathers may see themselves as less skilled 'mother substitutes', their contribution to children's care can be crucial. Men have been identified as primary carers in a minority of households throughout the post-war period; and the father is the parent with whom children live for most or all of the time in 10 per cent of families affected by divorce. Moreover, interviews with 33-year-olds whose lives have been followed since birth in 1958 by the National Child Development Study (NCDS) found that fathers were the main carers for children in 36 per cent of dual-earner families while mothers were working – more than any other individual.

Even in dual-earner families, or those where only the mother is in paid work, it is rare for fathers to identify themselves as the main carer. However, it is common for couples to say they take an equal share of being with and looking after their children. The NCDS interviews with 33-year-old parents found that most working and non-working fathers laid claim to an equal share of childcare, unless their partners stayed at home. Mothers were more sanguine about the contribution made by men, but 66 per cent of women working full time and 48 per cent of those working part time said the responsibilities were equally shared.

When questioned in theory about responsibility for childcare, middle-class parents tend to express more egalitarian attitudes than working-class parents. What happens in practice may be different. Among NCDS parents, only 35 per cent of fathers with graduate qualifications said they took an equal share of childcare, compared with 58 per cent of men with few or no qualifications.

Fathers at home

Today's parents have been shown to spend more time on average caring for their children than previous generations. Mothers are still more heavily involved in looking after children than fathers and also

continue to be chiefly responsible for the household chores (except for repairs and DIY). However, surveys show that fathers' involvement in the home has been increasing and that the 'gender gap' in terms of average time spent caring for children has narrowed. Fathers in many homes are reported to play a central role as playmates for younger children and as organisers of family activities. Interviews with the 33-year-old parents who were part of the NCDS found that fathers who were actively involved in childcare were also more likely to play out of doors with their children.

Further insight into what today's fathers do – and are expected to do – comes from a study of families with teenage children. It found that men's varied parenting activities ranged from providing discipline, helping with homework and acting as family chauffeur, to organising outings, shopping, acting as an opponent for computer games and watching or participating in sports. Mothers, children and fathers often described men's family role in terms of being 'involved' – a concept they found hard to define, but which appeared to include psychological availability as well as physically 'being there'.

Work, well-being and family involvement

Employment patterns explain much of men's involvement – or otherwise – inside the home. For example, seven out of ten mothers in the NCDS reported working outside the home in the evenings and about half worked at weekends. These patterns suggest that some mothers and fathers take it in turns to look after their children while the other is working. However, the extent of 'shift' parenting is not clear.

Generally speaking, the terms, conditions and expectations of paid employment stand as the greatest barrier to men's involvement in childcare. Across the European Union, 90 per cent of fathers are in paid jobs. In the United Kingdom, they work the longest hours of men in all the member states. One review found that the average working week for fathers of children aged under 11 was 48 hours. More than a quarter of the 33-year-old fathers in the NCDS were working 50 or more hours a week and almost a tenth worked more than 60 hours. Two-thirds regularly worked in the evening or at weekends and a third did night work. Women's average time commitment to paid employment was significantly smaller. Only a quarter of NCDS mothers worked more than 35 hours each week, while a third worked fewer than 16 hours.

Against that background, several studies have demonstrated that the more hours a father works, the less likely he is to contribute to childcare or to running the home. Men working long hours are also less likely to have a wife or partner who is in paid work, and they are more likely to express a view that the man's task is to earn a living for the family. Conversely, fathers are more likely to take responsibility for childcare if they are unemployed and their partners are working. Nevertheless, only 1 in 6 of the NCDS fathers in this situation reported taking the major share of childcare – outnumbered by the 1 in 5 who said their partner was mostly responsible.

The division of responsibilities within individual families can be expected to alter as children develop and their parents move into and out of the workforce. For example, older children as well as fathers in dual-earner households tend to contribute to domestic chores more than those in other families. Research suggests that the way domestic tasks are shared can not only affect personal relationships, but also relates to well-being. Dual-earner parents in the NCDS were more likely to go shopping and take part in other activities together. But parents in 'traditional' families where the father worked and the mother stayed at home reported slightly greater levels of marital satisfaction than other couples. Working mothers' discontent with partners who contributed little to the care and socialisation of their children tended to increase according to the number of hours that they themselves were working.

Yet there appeared to be little connection between men's sense of well-being and marital happiness and the extent of their involvement with

their children. Indeed, men working long hours and sharing childcare responsibilities with their partner tended to be least satisfied of all. One simple message that emerges from these contrasting research findings is that fathers, as well as mothers, find the combination of family responsibilities and a demanding job can be stressful.

Barriers to active fatherhood

Although clearly important, the amount of time men can spend at home when not working is not the only factor affecting their role in family life. Values and attitudes to parenthood also influence their involvement. For example, those who are less involved with their children appear to define fathering in terms of teaching 'good behaviour' rather than sharing outdoor recreation and other activities with them. The NCDS fathers, in households where they were the sole bread-winner, were generally less hands-on as parents and more likely to espouse 'traditional' beliefs concerning a disciplinary role.

Although most fathers play a substantial part in family life, it is important to consider why some do not. The range of different fathering 'relationships' revealed by recent research is in contrast with the 'traditional' pattern of fathers fitting family life around their paid work activities. Yet despite the increasingly 'hands-on' reality of modern fatherhood, cultural stereotypes concerning men as bread-winners remain powerful. The British Social Attitudes Survey continues to show that 53 per cent of fathers and 42 per cent of mothers agree with the belief that the father's role

is to 'provide'. Research for the Joseph Rowntree Foundation suggests that many teenagers of both sexes take the same view of men's contribution as parents.

This traditional view of fatherhood remains a major obstacle to any widespread acknowledgement that 'fathering' can be defined by childcare as well as economic provision. As a consequence:

- Young people more readily associate 'being a man' with 'having a job' and 'defending the family' than with 'being a good father'.
- Men who are not the main earners in their families, like mothers who stay at home with their children, receive little compensating recognition for their contribution to the social fabric as parents.

Fathers as well as mothers, in the study of families with teenage children, seemed to presume that women were better communicators, calmer, more patient and generally more sensitive to children's needs than men. The idea that women had a better understanding of 'the' way to parent a child was implicitly accepted. Mothers often said they preferred to look after children, to run the home and to serve as the link between the household and other family members. Indeed, there were families where mothers appeared to act as 'gatekeepers' to fathering, exerting control over the family and deciding when their partner's involvement was or was not required.

However, the barriers to active fathering are more than a matter of attitudes. As the evidence concerning long working hours makes plain, some men are prevented by their 'provider' role from spending as much time with their children as they would wish. A number of men in the study of families with teenagers expressed their resentment of uninteresting or poorly-paid jobs that left them with too little time for family life.

• The above is an extract from Foundations 440 – *A man's place in the home: Fathers and families in the UK*, produced by the Joseph Rowntree Foundation.

© Joseph Rowntree Foundation

Daddy's home . . .

In fact, he always is. There are 90,000 at-home dads in Britain, and even a senior Minister wants to be one. But it's not a soft option, says Ben Summerskill.

Most people have heard it at least once. Fuelled by a few glasses of chianti after a pleasant supper and in the private company of good friends, an old chum confides that he would love to give up work in order to devote more time to his children of whom he sees (a) not quite as much as he'd like, (b) far too little, or (c) frankly, almost nothing.

In the case of Alistair Darling, the wistful admission was made last week in the intimate confines of an interview with the *New Statesman*. 'Every Monday morning is an increasing wrench. It was OK at the start because there were no children... and then, when they're babies, they don't actually notice. But now there are times when I think that all I've got is access. The only solution is for me to stop what I'm doing,' he said.

The betting is that for all his fine words, the Social Security Secretary will be back at his Whitehall desk first thing tomorrow. And next week. And the week after.

Six months ago actor Jimmy Nesbitt disclosed that he too dreams of staying at home. The 35-year-old *Cold Feet* star, father to two-year-old Peggy, admitted: 'I think my real vocation would be being a full-time dad.'

Unlike Darling and Nesbitt, almost 90,000 British men have actually had the courage to give up their day-jobs. They have become 'at-home dads', a description they prefer to 'househusband', with all its loaded housewifely – and not very masculine – baggage of cleaning, ironing and shopping.

'But that is what I do,' says Hugh Gemmill, 41-year-old father of Josh and Sam, who has run the family home in Caversham, Berkshire, since 1996. 'Liz leaves at 6.45 each morning, then I get the boys sorted for school and nursery.

'I do shopping twice a week, once with Sam on a Tuesday. That's when we spend more time. He can look at the vegetables and measure things out. I do the bulk of it on Friday when he's at nursery and Josh is at school.'

'When they're both out of the house I can do DIY. I can also play football with them almost every day, or other sports. I'll do more of that as they get older.'

It was British social scientists who discovered some time ago that working-class men, in contrast to their expectations, did many more hours of childcaring than their middle-class counterparts. What the academics had overlooked, until they returned to their subjects to check, was that for people on lower incomes male involvement in childcaring, often while a mother works shifts, is an economic necessity and not a luxury.

'It's almost always true that primary care-giving fathers have a partner with a better job than they do,' says Dr Charlie Lewis, one of Britain's leading analysts of fatherhood. 'They actually have a choice.' Gemmill, for example, is lucky enough to be married to a successful senior IT manager with one of Britain's largest retailers.

'Men who do stay at home,' says Lewis, 'don't necessarily find it as easy as they expect. Research from abroad now shows that levels of satisfaction decline after a couple of years. It's not a simple life. For any parent, active parenting is a transient

---

In America, where the trend towards fathers as primary carers first started, the latest census showed 1.9 million fathers of children under 15 now define themselves as primary care-givers

---

phase. Women give up full-time work and then they filter back into the labour market.'

'There are definitely people around who are unsympathetic,' admits Gemmill. 'You get the feeling from them that you're not doing something meaningful.'

'There's no doubt that you lose a lot of your identity,' says Paul Giggle from Happisburgh in Norfolk, who gave up his job in engineering eight years ago, shortly after the birth of his fourth child. 'You lose your standing and status in life. Thankfully I'm fairly outgoing and extrovert, so the little asides in the playground didn't affect me.'

But Giggle's counterparts have shared the same experience. 'A father needs to plan some strategies to overcome the isolation he will feel,' says a spokeswoman for support group Parents at Work. 'He needs to make sure he has regular social activities.'

In America, where the trend towards fathers as primary carers first started, the latest census showed 1.9 million fathers of children under 15 now define themselves as primary care-givers. The figure is up from 400,000 30 years ago.

But US websites devoted to 'at-home dads' are littered with plaintive confidences. 'This is by far the most difficult job I've ever had to do,' admits Peter from Maine. 'It gets so lonely until my wife gets home,' says Brant from California. 'I need to communicate, if you know what I mean. Communication with children is fine, but I also need more intelligent life forms. My mother doesn't count.'

Andrew Cherlin, public policy professor at Johns Hopkins University in Maryland, acknowledges the difficulty these fathers face: 'Men who want to stay home and care for their children are fighting stereotypes as severe as women were fighting generations ago when they wanted to cross gender roles.'

Claire Rayner, who has advised millions of parents as a newspaper agony aunt, said: 'Men just have to stand up to the prejudices. Thirty years ago when I was a midwife it was considered wimpish if men wanted to come into labour wards. People will soon stop laughing at them if they want to be more active parents.'

Giggle, admitting to being more of a 'new man' than he used to be, says: 'My experience changed me and made my priorities very different.

Now that Charlie's at school full-time I've become a bus driver. I didn't want to return to the rat-race. But I also have a completely different relationship with my son. It's like being a brother, a mate. It's something that everyone should experience.'

But he concedes a downside too. 'You become a husk for the child. You're just there for his existence. I could never go out with friends. I couldn't play golf for four years. My life wasn't my own.

'If you know that someone is going out to work and keeping you sustained, you do anything to keep them comfortable. I knew my wife was the breadwinner. She'd come in and ask "Where's my bloody tea?" In the end I'd have a nice glass of wine waiting. Being a stay-home dad is a 24-hours-a-day, seven-days-a-week, 365-days-a-year job. It can be utterly exhausting.'

Just like being a stay-home mum, of course.

The world's women 2000

United Nations releases most recent statistics on the world's women. Latest comprehensive report on available data shows gains but persistent disparities between women and men worldwide.

The United Nations today released *The World's Women 2000: Trends and Statistics*, a one-of-a-kind compilation of the latest data documenting progress for women worldwide in six areas: health, human rights and political decision-making, work, education and communication, population, and families. The report, produced by the United Nations Statistics Division, becomes public just prior to a Special Session of the General Assembly to review progress governments have made in improving women's lives since the Fourth World Conference on Women in Beijing in 1995 and to agree on future priority actions for women.

'This report attempts to answer the urgent but complex question of what real progress are the world's women making in their lives,' said Nitin Desai, Under-Secretary-General for Economic and Social Affairs. 'Available data show that women are making gains, but persistent disparities exist between women and men. We can see that the gender gap in enrolment in primary and secondary levels of schooling is closing, but it is unlikely this gap will be closed by the target date of 2005. While the gender gap in rates of economic activity is narrowing, women still must reconcile their family responsibilities with employment outside the home.

Recent declines in early marriage and early childbearing in most regions show real change in the quality of women's lives, but in 3 of 5 countries in southern Asia and in 11 of 30 countries in sub-Saharan Africa, at least 30 per cent of young women aged 15 to 19 have been married.'

Citing progress in collecting gender statistics, the report also stresses that new data are needed on issues unique to women, such as violence against women and maternal health. For example, new importance is being placed on women's reproductive health and safe motherhood, but the report states that data are not yet available to show whether the new concern with safe motherhood has been translated into improved maternal care.

The World's Women 2000 is the third in a series of reports that has broken new ground. The first, issued in 1991, was a direct response to a rising demand by a wide range of users for data on women. The field continued to evolve with a second edition in 1995 and now the current edition that looks at the status of women through the lens of statistical data and analysis. The information and data in the present publication are intended to provide a 'snapshot' of some of the more salient statistical findings since 1995, while also drawing out recent changes and long-term trends.

In the last seven years, governments, institutions and non-governmental organisations have worked at every level to implement and incorporate the agendas of a series of UN conferences into national programmes for action. The success – or lack of success – of these efforts is the subject of *The World's Women 2000*. The topics within each field of concern were shaped both by the availability of data and by the calls for action emerging from the global conferences. Highlights and important findings in *The World's Women 2000* include:

Health

There are continuing differences in lifetime risk of maternal mortality between developed and developing countries. An African woman's lifetime risk of dying from pregnancy-related causes is 1 in 16; in Asia, 1 in 65; and in Europe, 1 in 1,400.

Women now account for almost half of all cases of HIV/AIDS, and in countries with high HIV prevalence, young women are at higher risk of contracting HIV than young men.

Life expectancy continues to increase for women and men in most developing regions but has decreased dramatically in Southern Africa as a result of AIDS.

Work

Women now comprise an increasing share of the world's labour force – at least one-third in all regions except in northern Africa and western Asia.

Self-employment and part-time and home-based work have expanded opportunities for women's participa-

---

Despite calls for gender and equality, women are significantly under-represented in governments, political parties and at the United Nations

---

tion in the labour force but are characterised by lack of security, lack of benefits and low income.

More women than before are in the labour force throughout their reproductive years, though obstacles to combining family responsibilities with employment persist.

Human rights and political decision-making

Physical and sexual abuse affect millions of girls and women worldwide – yet are known to be seriously under-reported.

In some African countries, more than half of all women and girls have undergone female genital mutilation and its prevalence is not declining.

Women and girls comprise half of the world's refugees and, as refugees, are particularly vulnerable to sexual violence while in flight, in refugee camps and/or during resettlement.

Despite calls for gender and equality, women are significantly under-represented in governments, in political parties and at the United Nations.

Education and communication

The gender gap in primary and secondary schooling is closing, but women still lag behind men in some countries in Africa and southern Asia.

Two-thirds of the world's 876 million illiterates are women, and the number of illiterates is not expected to decrease significantly in the next twenty years.

More women than men lack the basic literacy and computer skills needed to enter 'new media' professions.

Women and men in families

Women are generally marrying later but more than a quarter of women aged 15 to 19 are married in 22 countries – all in developing regions.

Informal unions are common in developed regions and in some countries of the developing regions.

Population

Women are having fewer children on average but with more women of reproductive age, world population continues to grow.

Women represent a large proportion of international migrants – an estimated 56 million women out of a total of 118 million migrants.

'Despite the fact that considerable progress has been made in the development of gender statistics, anecdote and misperception abound in measuring women's progress,' said Mr Desai. 'On many issues of particular concern, there is no data collected anywhere. On other relevant issues, data are collected but only in a few countries. Even basic statistical series on women are not collected routinely in many countries.

'The improvement of national statistical capacity – the ability to provide timely and reliable statistics – is essential for improving gender statistics. The United Nations Economic and Social Council has recognised the importance of statistical capacity building for the implementation and follow-up of the global conferences. It has urged countries, international and regional agencies to work together to create effective systems, especially in developing countries, to produce vital and necessary data so that we may truly understand women's advancement around the world.'

• *The World's Women 2000: Trends and Statistics* is available from United Nations Publications, Two UN Plaza, Room DC2-853, Dept. PRES, New York, NY 10017. Telephone: 800-253-9646 or 212-963-8302. Fax: 212-963-3489. E-mail: publications@un.org. Web site: www.un.org/publications

Work and the family today

Information from the National Family and Parenting Institute

At the beginning of the 21st century, more women work in paid employment than at any time during the last one hundred years. The majority of women spend a period working part-time when they have children. More men have flexible working patterns and more employers have adopted family-friendly work practices. Both men and women are more likely to change jobs or careers during their lifetime.

Full-time work

- Nearly 75% of adult men in the UK work.[8]
- In 1999 13.6 million men in the UK were working full-time.[8]
- Fathers in the UK work the longest hours in Europe – an average of 48 hours a week for those with children under 11 – and earn average two-thirds of the family income.[8]
- In 1999 three-quarters of women in the UK, living in a couple (married or cohabiting) and of working age, were employed.[1]
- In 1999 over 6 million women in the UK were working full-time.[8]
- Twenty per cent of women with dependent children work full-time.[8]

Part-time work

- In 1999 nearly one in 10 men in the UK were working part-time.[8]
- The number of men working part-time has doubled since 1984.[8]
- Forty per cent of men who work part-time do so because they do not want a full-time job.[8]
- In 1999 nearly 6 million women in the UK were working part-time.[8]
- In 1997 two-thirds of mothers with children under five were working part-time.[3]
- Eighty per cent of women who work part-time do so because they do not want a full-time job.[8]

- The International Labour Organisation predicts that in just over 10 years 80% of all women in western countries, including the UK, will combine employment with being a parent.[7]

Flexible working

- Women are more likely than men to have flexible working patterns. In 1999, nearly 25% of female full-time employees in the UK had flexible working patterns and about 15% of men. The most common form of flexible working was flexi-time, for women and men. For women who work part-time, the most common form of flexible working is term-time only hours, including teachers.[8]

The most common form of flexible working was flexi-time, for women and men

---

Unpaid work

- Women spend an average of four and a half hours a day doing unpaid work – childcare and household chores.[8]
- Men spend an average of nearly three hours a day doing unpaid work – childcare and household chores.[8]

Maternity and childcare

- The numbers of women aged between 35 and 39 having a baby doubled in the 1980s and 1990s.[2]
- Projections suggest that one in four women born in 1972 will be childless at age 45.[2]
- No official figures for the take-up or length of maternity leave are available. Preliminary findings from an Economic and Social Research Council study taking place at Kent University into how women make decisions about work and childcare after the birth of a first child show that although 60% of women who intended to return to work full-time did so by the time their

babies were six months, the overall trend is for women to do less work than they intended to after the birth of heir first child.[6]

- Nearly half of all parents of pre-school children use day-care in term-time.[2]
- Nearly one in five pre-school children are looked after by relatives.[5]
- Nearly one in four pre-school children attend nurseries, playgroups or parent and toddler groups.[5]
- Nearly a third of all children aged 4-13 use care after school.[2]
- The National Childcare Strategy was launched in May 1998 and aims to provide childcare places for children up to 14 years (or 16 years for children with special needs) in every area.[2]

Finding out more about the family and work

This information summarises the key facts about work and family life in the UK today in an at-a-glance format. Most of the information included comes from government sources or charitable foundations. There is little information available about the take-up of maternity and paternity benefits, or about how parents change their working patterns, or make career changes to fit in with family life.

References

1   *Annual Abstract of Statistics 2000*, Office for National Statistics

2   *Britain 2000, The Official Yearbook of the United Kingdom*, Office for National Statistics, 2000

3   *Labour Force Survey*, Office for National Statistics, 1997

4   Charlie Lewis, *Fathers and Families in the UK*, Foundations: Joseph Rowntree Foundation, April 2000

5   *Living in Britain: Results from the 1998 General Household Survey*, Office for National Statistics Social Survey Division, 2000.

6   *Maternity Action*, Maternity Alliance Newsletter, Winter 2000

7   New South Wales Department of Industrial Relations Briefing, 2000

8   *Social Trends 30*, Office for National Statistics, The Stationery Office, 2000.

The work-life balance

Information from the Equal Opportunities Commission (EOC)

In the past men usually went out to work and were the sole bread-winners while women stayed at home to look after the family and home. This has now changed radically as more women have entered the workforce. There is now a mismatch between people's caring and parenting responsibilities and the demands of inflexible employment patterns.

While it is still the case that most mothers take a greater responsibility for the care of children than fathers, they are also more likely to be in employment than ever before. Conversely, the role of fathers and their need for time for parenting is beginning to be recognised and accepted. At the other end of the spectrum, greater longevity means more people are in need of care as frailty and illness take their toll.

During the course of their working life the family and marital status of many employees will change, some-times dramatically, reflecting the more fluid and diverse family patterns which have evolved. The working environment needs to adapt to these changes if it is to retain skilled, experienced people. The work-life balance aims to create a

EQUAL OPPORTUNITIES COMMISSION

closer fit between employment practices and people's needs especially for those with parenting and caring responsibilities.

Employment rates and hours of work are closely related to parental and caring responsibilities. For mothers, these are lower than for women without children. For fathers the opposite applies – men with

children are more likely to be working longer hours than men without children. Carers and parents can make a vital contribution at work provided there is sufficient flexibility to enable them to meet their responsibilities.

The EOC sees the work-life balance as central to equality for women and men. The EOC has been active in this area for many years, using both its law enforcement and promotional powers to encourage change. The development of a childcare infrastructure, improvements to statutory maternity leave and the introduction of parental leave will have a beneficial effect but much more needs to be done to help people balance their family and working lives more comfortably.

The EOC is calling for: the introduction of paid parental leave; wider opportunities for part-time or new ways of work-ing; a reduction in long hours working; more encouragement for men to take an active role in parenting; and greater protection from discrimination for carers and others with family responsibilities.

Sex discrimination

Information from the Industrial Society

Definition

Sex discrimination at work, under the Sex Discrimination Act 1975, means discriminating on the grounds of sex or marital status in terms of:

- recruitment and selection;
- terms and conditions of employment offered and provided;
- access to promotion, transfers and training;
- other benefits and services;
- dismissal; and
- subjecting the person to any other detriment.

Background

The Sex Discrimination Act 1975 followed equal pay legislation in 1970 and the EEC's Equal Treatment Directive of 1975.

The Sex Discrimination Act 1986 removed restrictions on women working shift work and nights.

The exception to the Sex Discrimination Act is when there is a Genuine Occupational Qualification (GOQ). A GOQ can apply in either of two ways:

- physiology or authenticity, for instance hiring a model for women's clothes; or
- decency and privacy, for people working abroad where another culture's customs or laws restrict the ability of one sex to work effectively.

Possible remedies include:

- if a woman or man complains of discrimination, she or he can take an employer to an industrial tribunal and may be awarded damages; or
- the Equal Opportunities Commission (EOC) may do the same, and may also investigate organisations it believes to be discriminating.

Discrimination may be direct, when people are treated less favourably because of their sex.

It may also be indirect, when the conditions of employment make it more difficult for members of one sex to comply. The conditions may be fair in principle, but discriminatory in effect.

Deliberate segregation by sex is unlawful.

Victimisation is also unlawful, for example when a person faces disciplinary action or dismissal as a result of bringing a complaint under the Act.

Protection under the Act applies to all employees, regardless of length of service or hours.

Key facts

Since 1993, the ceiling on compensation in sex discrimination cases has been abolished.

The EOC helped applicants in discrimination cases to win a total of £711,832. Out of 71 cases last year, ten were successful, 19 were unsuccessful and 42 were settled outside court.

In those the cases that were settled, half the employers have agreed to change policies and practices.

Three-quarters of complaints were from women, and there has been an increase in the number of women complaining that they are denied access to training.

The EOC says women are paid, on average, 20% less than men, with fewer opportunities to take up overtime, shiftwork and bonuses.

Women who work part-time earn less than half the hourly pay of male part-timers.

There is still discrimination against men who want to work in traditional women's work.

The proportion of women in the workforce is growing faster than men. From 1994 to 2001, the numbers of women and men being 'economically active' will grow by 11% and 3% respectively. Current figures are 71% of women of working age and 85% of men.

44% of women work part-time and only 6% of men, but this rate is increasing twice as fast as that of women.

State of play

Opportunity 2000, a group of employers committed to promoting opportunities for women at all levels, has produced its fifth year progress report, with many companies showing how they have increased the numbers and percentage of women in higher levels of management. It includes:

- Abbey National, which has 53%

Fair pay for women now!

Statistics on women and pay. Basic statistics on women and pay make depressing reading:

- Full-time women employees earn 81 pence for every £1 earned by full-time male employees [1]
- Part-time women employees earn 60 pence for every £1 earned by full-time male employees [2]
- 20% of women full-time employees earn less than £200 per week, compared with 8% of male full-time employees [3]
- Only 26% of part-time women employees are members of occupational pension schemes, compared with 53% of full-time women employees and 58% of full-time male employees [4]
- Statutory Maternity Pay in the UK is equivalent to 8.6 weeks at full pay, compared with the European Union average of 22 weeks at full pay [5]
- There is no right to payment for parental leave in the UK. Some payment for parental leave is available in ten out of fifteen European Union member states [6]

The gender pay gap in average hourly earnings for full-time women employees compared with male full-time employees has narrowed substantially since the mid-1970s, although remaining static at around 80% for the latter part of the 1990s. Until 1999 the difference in hourly earnings between women who work part-time and men who work full-time had not altered significantly since the mid-1970s.

But the largest narrowing for almost a decade in both the full-time and part-time gender hourly pay gap has been due to the introduction of the National Minimum Wage in April 1999. In particular, the average hourly pay for part-time women employees increased significantly more rapidly than for full-time women employees. The Low Pay Commission has calculated that over two-thirds of the beneficiaries of the NMW are women. Of whom two-thirds work part-time [7].

[1] New Earnings Survey, 1999. [2] Supra, note 2. [3] see 'the Gender Pay Gap', IDS Report 799, December 1999. [4] General Household Survey 1996. [5] See 'Reconciliation between work and family life', European Commission, 1998, at p.7. [6] See evidence given by Professor Peter Moss to the House of Commons Social Security Committee enquiry on parental leave, October 1999, at p.96. [7] The National Minimum Wage – the Story so far, Low Pay Commission, February 2000, at p.16.

Source: Trades Union Congress

- of branch managers and 43% of senior managers who are women;
- the Benefits Agency has 46% of middle managers who are women and 30% at board level; and
- a third of Northern Foods' workforce and managers are women, although mostly in lower managerial grades.

An IDS study on Opportunity 2000 found that the most important factors in success were:
- commitment from senior management;
- ownership of equal opportunities from line managers;
- incremental change; and
- maintaining the momentum.

Best practice guidelines

Employers need the best people for jobs and they need to reflect the diversity of the community in terms of sex, race, age, disability, etc. This can help in dealing with customers, proving good corporate citizenship and using all talents to the full.

Policies and practices should ensure that all employees are aware that it is against the law to discriminate.

Those responsible for recruitment, access to training, appraisal and promotion should be trained to avoid sexist assumptions and stereotyping, for instance that customers/ suppliers would not accept a woman, and that women would not want that job or be strong enough to do it.

Selection criteria should be reviewed to ensure they do not contain unnecessary qualifications or requirements. Women should not be asked about their marital status or plans to have children unless men are also asked and there is a role-related reason to ask.

Job adverts, external as well as in-house, are more likely to ensure diversity and fair employment than word of mouth, which generally replicates the existing workforce.

Keep records for all stages of recruitment and promotion so that lack of bias can be proved. Record the sex of all applicants for jobs and promotion.

Retirement ages and terms should be the same for all in the same category regardless of sex.

Employers can encourage and train women to prepare them for work in areas where they are under-represented.

Dress codes should be justifiable and have the same impact on both sexes.

© The Industrial Society

Mothers versus men

Why women lose at work

Introduction

The future, just in case you missed the news, is female. On this point business gurus, feminists, pollsters, psychologists and scientists agree. Changes in the world of work mean that 'male' attributes are becoming a hindrance; women's 'softer' skills are the order of the day. Girls outperform boys at school, securing more A grades at A-level, and graduate from law and medical schools in higher numbers.

Men are said to be facing an age of 'reproductive redundancy'. Lone parenthood has lost its stigma. US scientists perfect a technique for turning DNA from two eggs into a viable embryo and women's magazines ask, post-IVF, 'Who Needs Men?' Men are three times more likely to kill themselves, die on average five years younger, suffer more mental distress following divorce etc., etc. You've heard all this.

But it is largely nonsense. A few well-paid women and a couple of chemistry experiments do not make a revolution. And nowhere is the claim of the new female superiority more overstated than in relation to paid work. Men are still paid, promoted and trained more than women. The pay gap, stuck at 20 per cent, belies all the hype about an Amazonian future.

The reasons why women still lose at work is simple: they have children. Of course men have children too, but it doesn't matter much – while for women, it matters a great deal. Taking time out of the labour market, deciding to work part-time and rushing home to care for a sick child all dent earning potential. Right now it is only women's pay packets being hit, because none of the above applies to fathers.

Employers discriminate against women, and with good reason. Women are riskier appointments than men, because of the chance they will have children. It is illegal, of course, but perfectly rational. It is about time we admitted as much.

Tinkering around the edges of the gender gap with modest improvements in paternity leave and exhortations to employers to be more flexible won't do any harm. But it won't do much good either. Only when fathers and mothers bear equal responsibility for parenting can men and women share equal status at work. This is simply an economic fact of life, one which no amount of rhetoric or campaigning will alter.

When the phrases 'career man' or 'working father' have ceased to sound silly, when a man carrying a baby on a Tuesday afternoon is not gawped at, when breadwinning is not seen as a strand of the Y chromosome, women will have a shot at equal status in the office and boardroom. Not before.

- The above information is the introduction of *Mothers versus men: why women lose at work*, a publication produced by the Industrial Society by Richard Reeves, which calls for paternity and maternity rights to be equalised, arguing that women's prime responsibility for parenting makes it rational for employers to discriminate against them. ISBN: 1 85835 994 5. Published: August 2000 priced at £20.00.

© The Industrial Society 2000

Will women always be second in the workplace?

Yes, says Richard Reeves of the Industrial Society. Only when men bear equal responsibility for parenting will women have a shot at equality. But Ruth Lea, head of the policy unit at the Institute of Directors, argues that the allocation of extensive paternity leave would be disruptive and unnecessary.

Dear Ruth,

It is a quarter of a century since the Equal Pay Act, but women still earn only 80 pence for every pound pocketed by men. There have been scores of initiatives to help women break through the corporate glass ceiling, but just 3% of directors are female. But of course, you know all this.

It is not because women are less educated or skilled – look at last week's A-level results – or because employers think women aren't up to the job, or because women are uninterested in jobs or money. Twentysomething female graduates earn as much as their male counterparts. Women continue to lose at work because they have children, and so their career paths are broken. Men have children and continue working as if nothing had happened.

We either accept the resulting gap in pay and promotion, as conservatives do, or level the playing field. My view is that we have to give men the same rights to paid time off for childcare as women (44 weeks, with the first six paid at 90% wages).

Only when men bear equal responsibility for parenting will women have a shot at equality. Not before.

Yours sincerely,
Richard Reeves
The Industrial Society

Dear Richard

I found your proposals suggesting that men should bear equal responsibility for parenting very interesting. I do have objections. Your statement that

---

Women continue to lose at work because they have children, and so their career paths are broken. Men have children and continue working as if nothing had happened

---

women continue to lose at work because they have career breaks, while true, implies that all women define their success in life mainly in terms of careers and not in terms of motherhood. For many women this is not true. Many of my friends were only too pleased to give up work and look after their children.

They feel insulted when this is seen as less important or prestigious than having a job, which can be tedious, unrewarding and unglamorous. They regard bringing up their children as the finest thing they have ever done.

Men are different from women and women are on the whole psychologically and biologically better equipped to be the principal child nurturers. A recent report by a Lancaster University psychology professor concluded that most fathers saw their parental role as protector and breadwinner and preferred to leave nurturing to their womenfolk. This may be a non-PC view. But men should be given an opportunity to behave as they feel in this matter without being criticised.

If men took as much leave as women over the birth of a baby, the disruption to many firms (especially

small ones) would be horrendous and increase the resentment by the childless towards those, especially women, with children.

A recent report in *Management Today* suggested that such resentment was growing.

Yours sincerely,
Ruth Lea
Head of the Policy Unit,
Institute of Directors

Dear Ruth,
You have cut straight to the heart of the matter. But I could not agree with you less. Yes, many women are happy to devote themselves to their families. But so are many men; they are denied the opportunity to do so. I am not arguing that bringing up children is an unimportant job. I am arguing that it is too important for just one parent.

Women are not naturally better at looking after children than men – they just do more of it. Given the chance, men acquire childcare skills as quickly as women. It is true that today most people support a fairly traditional division of labour. But attitudes change. A few decades ago, working mothers of young children faced widespread disapproval. Employers will face disruption when fathers take time off, exactly as they currently do with mothers. But every move to give workers more time off – from shorter working days to maternity leave – has been seen as a threat to profits. Capitalism seems to have survived. Even if there is a cost, this is far outweighed by the benefits to men, children and, most of all, to women.

Yours,
Richard

Dear Richard
Many fathers are devoted to their families. But the survey I quoted, by psychology professor Charlie Lewis, stated that most fathers see their main duty as bringing in money while mothers look after their children. This is particularly the case when the child is very young. This would suggest that the take-up rate for men for paternity leave over the first months of a child's life would be low.

I do not believe that men have the same instinctive parenting skills

as women. There are exceptions to every generalisation. But exceptions do not overturn the basic differences between men and women in the reproductive process. This may be regarded as hopelessly reactionary, but to deny it is to deny the essence of what distinguishes men from women. I am not as sanguine about the impact on businesses as you are concerning yet more regulations. The current government has, for its own social engineering agenda, introduced extra employment regulations that create serious problems. Even though I speculate that the take-up for paternity leave would be low, I stick to the view that such leave could prove devastating for small businesses already being strangled in red tape.

Yours,
Ruth

Dear Ruth,
Your two arguments contradict each other. If men are not interested in childcare, and so will not take up paid paternity leave, how will it be devastating for business?

Men are rethinking their role as fathers – young men rank loving your

---

Men are different from women and women are on the whole psychologically and biologically better equipped to be the principal child nurturers

---

child and being responsible ahead of breadwinning. Nor do women have instinctively better parenting skills than men – that is simply a stereotype underpinned by law. I agree that we are a long way, as a society, from seeing this. But in a few decades' time your view will seem as outdated as the one that women aren't really up to the rigours of paid labour. The only significant biological difference is that women can breastfeed – and I imagine most couples would use the mother's leave in the first months, with the father taking over if she returns to work. The need for childcare does not end with the need for breast milk.

My proposals to give men the same rights as women are about choice. If men don't want to take time off, so be it. But I think they will and I think their partners will want them to. Employed women could then compete with their male colleagues on equal terms.

Yours,
Richard

Dear Richard
I think it is very clear that the amount of disruption to individual businesses would be conditional on the take-up rate. If many men did take the leave, the difficulties for businesses would be significant and could then stimulate the backlash by the childless against parents. You talk of extending choice. But your proposals are only for the parents of young children.

I am not surprised to see young men rank loving their children ahead of breadwinning. But this doesn't mean they wish to do the nurturing. Your points that women do not have better parenting instincts than men and that the only biological difference is that women breastfeed, left me gasping. That a woman carries the baby and gives birth colours attitudes. Why do women usually get custody after divorce cases? No amount of paternity leave can change this.

And neither should it.

Yours,
Ruth

• First published in *The Guardian*, August 2000.

© *Ruth Lea and Richard Reeves*

Valuing women

The campaign for equal pay

EQUAL OPPORTUNITIES COMMISSION

The gap between men's pay and women's pay is a major source of inequality between women and men. Whichever way you look at the data on pay, women's average earnings are lower than those of men: women are receiving only 80% of men's hourly earnings. Britain's equal pay record when compared to other European countries is poor – tenth out of fifteen countries surveyed.

The pay gap affects women throughout their lives and is found in all industries and occupations. Closing the pay gap is the EOC's top priority for the next three years, through our new campaign – Valuing Women.

What is Valuing Women about?

The aim of Valuing Women is to eliminate those elements of the pay gap between women and men that are due to sex discrimination in payment systems. We want to see all employers taking action that will help achieve this.

To make this possible, in the short term the EOC's Valuing Women campaign aims to:
- Raise public and business awareness of the pay gap and the benefits of getting rid of it.
- Involve leaders of organisations across society in working with us to find solutions to the problem of unequal pay.
- Provide practical support to those committed to tackling unequal pay.

Although the original Equal Pay Act of 1970 was followed by a rapid narrowing of the pay gap, our experience since is that the gap remains obstinately stuck and has narrowed little in recent years. But there is no reason why the pay gap should not be eliminated within a few years if employers acted now, conducting pay audits to identify the problems and then developing and implementing the appropriate solutions.

Closing the pay gap will be good for individuals, good for businesses, and good for Britain.

Proper rewards for the jobs held by women will build fairness into our society and give due recognition to the caring roles currently undertaken largely by women.

Because more women work in lower paid jobs, equal pay for women will make a significant contribution to ending child poverty.

And equal pay will help women to realise their full potential by creating a level playing field in the workplace between women and men.

Taken overall, equal pay will help to break the vicious cycle of a lifetime of inequality where women's lower earnings result in greater poverty in old age. Equal pay will make it easier for women to make provision for their old age.

For employers, equal pay is essential to fairness at work:
- Pay systems that are simple, transparent and easy to understand send a positive message to the workforce about the value an organisation puts on its staff.
- Pay reviews avoid unfair discrimination and ensure that the skills, experience and potential of all staff are rewarded fairly, thereby increasing the organisation's morale, efficiency, productivity and competitiveness.

Equal pay is about good management. Ultimately, if employers do not reward talent fairly, good employees will not stay with their company. We know that young people expect equal pay, and many young women and men may choose not to work for a company which gives women less reward for their contribution to its success.

Tackling unequal pay: why now?

We believe that equal pay is an issue whose time has come. As we move towards a new century, there are many indicators that our attitudes to pay are changing.

Attitude surveys commissioned by the EOC show that young people of both sexes expect women to receive equal pay with men. They are shocked at the pay disparity that exists even at the age of 20. 'Women's rates', however well disguised, are unacceptable.

Since 1995 the number of equal pay cases registered with employment tribunals has more than doubled.

Government initiatives such as the National Minimum Wage and the forthcoming guarantee of equal treatment for part-time workers should lead to a substantial improvement in the rates of pay of the lowest paid women.

Major public sector employers such as the health service and local government are showing the way by adapting their own payment systems to meet the expectations of a modern workforce. The Bett's Committee Report on pay in Higher Education looked specifically at the issue of equal pay, and research has also been conducted by the Law Society, and by the British Film Institute.

Trade unions are playing a major part in securing equal pay for their women members and in negotiating new payment systems which recognise and reward women's worth.

It's clear that the time for a campaign to close the pay gap has come.

Tackling the pay gap cannot be achieved by the EOC alone. We all need to take action if it is to be eliminated.

Employers – far too few employers audit their pay systems for sex bias. We want employers to do pay audits, as suggested in the EOC's Code of Practice on Equal Pay, so that they know what the rates of pay are for their employees by sex and by hours worked and can find out for themselves what proportion of the pay gap is due to sex discrimination in their payments systems.

Individuals and trade unions – can ask for a pay audit. We want to see all trade unions putting the conduct of a pay audit and action to eliminate the pay gap at the centre of the bargaining agenda. Differentials based on gender are not acceptable.

Government – the complicated nature of the law makes it difficult for people to follow. We want the right to equal pay to be easily understood and easily enforced. We want employers to know where they stand. We should like to see legislation made more effective by:

- amending tribunal proceedings
- setting a standard for all Government suppliers to demonstrate that they provide equal pay by doing a pay audit and following the EOC Code of Practice
- discussing a time limit for the voluntary approach to monitoring pay, and taking action to enforce monitoring if the voluntary approach does not work
- giving tribunals powers to make general findings and recommendations and to make changes to collective agreements

The Government also has a vital role to play as an employer, conducting pay audits in the NHS and Civil Service.

Valuing Women: what the EOC will do to support you

We will:

- Stop pay discrimination being hidden – we will make sure that people are aware of the reality of unfair pay through research, publications and campaigning.
- Involve those who can make a difference in finding the practical solutions; our Task Force brings together key employers, pay specialists and trade unions. They will work together to investigate, make practical recommendations and set a target date for eliminating the pay gap. Their recommendations will include suggestions which will make the law easier to understand and use.

- Make it easier for employees to obtain equal pay. We will continue to provide guidance for those seeking advice on how to make a claim, and will produce a simple guide to tribunal proceedings. We will work with trade unions to spread good practice, and continue to use our enforcement powers to obtain fair pay for individuals and tackle discrimination through use of our formal investigative powers. We will also promote the case for legal reform to make the law easier to use.
- Make it easier for employers to act. Our Code of Practice on Equal Pay contains simple guidelines for employers, and we shall continue to promote this. We will facilitate our employers' group to identify and develop good practice which can be promoted through the EOC's equality exchange and other mechanisms. We will also promote the case for legal reform to make the law easier to understand and less time consuming.
- Raise awareness through different industries. The pay gap varies in different sectors of employment. We shall work with employers, trade unions and trade associations in each sector, to develop good practice and ways of closing the pay gap.

And finally. We want to work with you. We have set up the 'Valuing Women' website in order to post regular information and updates on the campaign. And we have an e-mail address: Valuing.Women@eoc.org.uk.

© Equal Opportunities Commission

Fair pay for women workers

The TUC is campaigning for fair pay for women workers

Did you know that UK working women are still being undervalued . . .

- Full-time women employees earn 81 pence for every £1 earned by full-time male employees
- Part-time women employees earn 60 pence for every £1 earned by full-time male employees
- 20% of women employees earn less than £200 per week, compared with only 8% of male full-time employees
- Only one in four part-time women employees are members of employers' pension schemes, compared with nearly two out of three full-time male employees
- Women from some ethnic minority groups, especially Pakistani and Bangladeshi or Indian women, are especially badly paid in comparison with men and with other women
- UK women who have children lose much more of their lifetime earnings than comparable women in six other major industrialised countries
- Statutory Maternity Pay in the UK works out at only 9 weeks at full pay, the lowest rate in the European Union
- There is no right to payment for parental leave in the UK. Some payment for parental leave is available in ten out of the fifteen EU member states

But women get fairer treatment if they are in unions. Women in unions earn on average nearly 90% of the hourly pay of their male counterparts. Non-unionised women earn on average only two-thirds of the hourly rate of non-unionised men.

And all the important legal victories in equal pay cases have been won by unions. Most recently, in May 2000:

- MSF settled a 13-year case involving hundreds of speech therapists. The final payouts came to £12 million.
- Six unions won a European case giving compensation for discrimination in pensions for thousands of part-time women workers. *© TUC*

Young people's attitudes to, and awareness of, equal pay

Information from the Equal Opportunities Commission (EOC)

The EOC commissioned NOP to examine how aware students are of the inequality in earnings between women and men and to find out whether this is an issue of major concern to them.

Key findings

- Before being told about it, awareness of the gender pay gap was low amongst all students.
- 60 per cent thought that men and women with the same qualifications and doing the same jobs would earn the same pay.
- The great majority of students expected to have the same earnings in five and ten years as those of the opposite sex who had similar experience and did the same jobs.
- When told about the pay gap, 76 per cent of women and 60 per cent of men stated that it was unfair.
- Very few students found the pay gap acceptable. Women were more likely to be disappointed, angry and shocked, whereas men were more likely to be surprised.
- There was almost universal agreement that women and men should be paid the same salary for carrying out the same job.
- 50 per cent of female students stated that the existence of the pay gap would make them re-consider their choice of job.
- 49 per cent of all students stated that the commitment of an employer to provide equal pay would influence their choice of job. Women were more likely than men to hold this view.
- 64 per cent considered that the UK Government should have responsibility for ensuring equal pay for women and men at work. 45 per cent stated that this was the responsibility of employers and companies.

EQUAL OPPORTUNITIES COMMISSION

Views about the gender pay gap

Before being told about it, awareness of the gender pay gap was low amongst all students. 60 per cent considered that men and women with the same qualifications and doing the same jobs would earn the same pay: 'women used to get less pay, now it's the same as men.'

A higher proportion of male (69 per cent) than female (53 per cent) students held this view; younger and FE/sixth form students were more likely to do so than older and HE students.

Students were shown average pay levels of those with similar qualifications as themselves. Nine out of ten identified that average earnings were higher for men than for women. 76 per cent of women and 60 per cent of men thought this was unfair. Very few students found the pay gap acceptable: 'didn't realise it would be so much'.

Women were more likely to be disappointed, angry and shocked by the figures, whereas men were more likely to be surprised: 'those figures astonish me'.

There was almost universal agreement that women and men should be paid the same salary for carrying out the same job. Only 2 per cent of students disagreed with this view.

The pay gap and future employment

50 per cent of female students, but only 17 per cent of male students, stated that the existence of the pay gap would make them reconsider their choice of job.

49 per cent of all students stated that the commitment of an employer to provide equal pay would influence their choice of job. Women (71 per

---

The gender pay gap

Attitudes to equal pay. Respondents were asked to choose up to three words which described their reaction to the pay gap

■ Men ▨ Women

Acceptable · Anger · Expected · Disappointed · Unfair

Source: Equal Opportunities Commission (EOC)

cent) were much more likely than men (23 per cent) to hold this view. Men were more likely than women to state that their choice of job would not be influenced by this factor.

The main reasons given by students for agreeing with this statement were that women should receive the same pay as men for the same job or the same qualifications and that there should be equal opportunities/equal rights.

Pay gap solutions

Students were asked to indicate how best to make young people more aware of equal pay.

44 per cent considered that a wide-scale media campaign was the best option. 24 per cent preferred the publication of figures showing inequality in pay. 14 per cent favoured publicity by colleges and 13 per cent considered that employers should provide their pay rates for men and women in their careers literature.

Students were also asked to state (with more than one choice) who should have responsibility for ensuring equal pay for women and men at work.

64 per cent considered this to be the responsibility of the UK Government: 'women come into government, they have their own voice, they can do something'.

45 per cent mentioned employers and companies. 29 per cent mentioned the EOC. Women were more likely than men to refer to the Government and to employers.

Retirement and pensions

Nine out of ten students considered that when men and women retire from similar careers, they should have the same amount to live on; a higher proportion of women (96 per cent) than men (88 per cent) held this view.

80 per cent of students considered that men and women with the same qualifications and doing the same jobs should receive equal pensions. Women (87 per cent) were more likely than men (71 per cent) to hold this view.

Methodology

The research covered students in higher education (HE), further education (FE) and sixth form colleges who were expecting to obtain full-time employment in the year 2000.

Four focus groups were conducted in one locality in August 1999, two with HE and two with FE/sixth form students. This was followed by face-to-face interviews in September 1999 in five localities across Britain with 398 students (217 women and 181 men) aged 17-24. Half the sample were HE students and a quarter each were FE and sixth form students.

© Equal Opportunities Commission (EOC)

Equal pay and low pay campaign

Information from the Fawcett Society

Women's low pay: the problem

'Women's' work – the jobs that are traditionally carried out by women – is low paid and undervalued. Women still earn only 79% of men's pay. In every industry and at every level, from the lowest paid to the highest, women earn less than men.

The gap between men's and women's earnings is even greater in lower paid jobs in which women are concentrated; with women manual workers earning on average 27% less than male manual workers. In fact women are twice as likely as men to be low paid.

Why are women badly paid?

The work traditionally done by women has been consistently undervalued. It has been argued that these jobs, often low paid and part time, suit the needs of women. This argument is based on a series of misconceptions about the nature of 'women's work'.

Five misconceptions about women's work

1. Women's work is low skilled and that is why it is low paid.
Men and women still tend to work in different jobs. Women are more

---

The gap between men's and women's earnings is even greater in lower paid jobs in which women are concentrated

---

likely than men to work in sectors like catering, cleaning and caring, doing work which is similar to their traditional work in the home. They also work in manufacturing where 'nimble fingers' are needed. These areas of work are regarded as low skilled and are low paid because:
- they are similar to the work which women do 'naturally' at home,
- 'male' qualities such as physical strength have been given a higher value than 'female' qualities such as emotional strength,
- women and men are paid in different ways – women are less likely to receive shift payments or overtime and are more likely than men to be classified as part-time,
- women are less likely to be in a union than men and many low-

paid women work in jobs where very few people are in unions.

2. Women prefer low-paid part-time work as it fits in with their home responsibilities.

Many women do not have a choice in the type of work they take. Most women are unhappy with their low pay, but need the money. A lack of childcare means that many women are forced to take on this type of work.

3. Women feel they get the pay they deserve.

Most women are unhappy with the pay and status of their jobs. Between 1990 and 1994 over 2,000 cases seeking 'equal pay for work of equal value' have been taken to industrial tribunals. This is despite the fact that 'equal value' cases are notoriously complicated and lengthy and take an average of two and a half years to go through the system, with some important cases having run for over nine years!

4. Women's wages are not important to the household income, they just work for 'pin money'.

The wages that women earn are essential to the household income. Without the woman's contribution the number living in poverty would increase by 50%.

What has been done?

The 1970 Equal Pay Act and the 1975 Sex Discrimination Act addressed direct discrimination in the workplace where women were refused jobs because of their sex, or where women were paid less than men for doing the same job.

The 1984 Equal Pay Act introduced the clause of 'equal pay for work of equal value'. This means that a woman can claim equal pay with a man (or a man with a woman), where she is working for the same employer doing work which is 'of equal value', for example using similar skills or skills of equal value.

Many employers have carried out 'job revaluation schemes' to comply with the 1984 Act. These schemes should examine the jobs of all employees and give each one a

EQUAL PAY NOW!

'value'. However, many of the revaluation schemes have continued to give a low value and status to the skills needed for 'women's jobs'.

It takes a long time to bring a case for equal pay for work of equal value and claims can be difficult to prove. The law favours the employer.

Despite this over 2,000 cases seeking 'equal pay for work of equal value' have been won at industrial tribunals between 1990 and 1994. For every high profile case there are countless others which receive out-of-court settlements.

Three examples of successful cases:

1. Nursery nurses in Gloucestershire won a case in an industrial tribunal where they claimed their work was equal to that of a Council waste technician or architectural technician. Their salaries should be increased by over £5,000 a year. This was despite the fact that they were entitled to more leave.

The wages that women earn are essential to the household income. Without the woman's contribution the number living in poverty would increase by 50%

---

2. A canteen cook who argued she was worth the same as a painter, a joiner or a thermal engineer won her case. She won equal pay although she had better conditions than the men.

3. A checkout operator had her job compared to a warehouse worker. She won equal pay which resulted in all the firm's checkout operators gaining £17 extra a week. As a result of this case another major retailer increased the pay of its sales staff by £31.50 a week to equal the rates of the warehouse workers.

Equal Opportunities Commission Code of Practice

The Equal Opportunities Commission (EOC) have produced a Code of Practice with the aim of helping companies to re-evaluate the work and the pay rates of their employees. A government commitment to implement the code for their own employees would help to introduce its widespread use.

What can be done?

Over twenty years have passed since the Equal Pay Act was introduced and the Equal Opportunities Commission was set up. Women's work continues to be undervalued and low paid.

Even when companies have carried out job revaluation schemes, all too often the status quo is reinforced because the value attached to women's work is not questioned.

Fawcett is calling for:

Reform of the equal pay legislation
A commitment to strengthen the Equal Pay Act, including making it easier for women to take cases to industrial tribunals.

A revaluation of women's work
Work traditionally done by women has always been undervalued. We need to revalue traditional 'women's jobs' to ensure women get the pay they deserve.

• The above information is from the Fawcett Society, see page 41 for their address details.

© Fawcett Society

Women make inroads into top jobs

Information from the Institute of Management (IM)

Women are staking their claim in the business world, holding almost three times as many managerial roles as a decade ago. Women executives are also closing the gender pay gap, lagging only 8 per cent in their salaries contrasted to 38 per cent in 1990.

According to the National Management Salary Survey 2000, released by the Institute of Management (IM) and Remuneration Economics, almost a quarter (22 per cent) of managers today are women – a great leap from only 8 per cent in 1990. Women have also muscled their way into the boardroom to a small but growing presence of 9.6 per cent from a mere 1.6 per cent ten years ago.

In the last year, female managers have once again outperformed their male counterparts in the salary stakes to receive, on average, 19 per cent higher pay increases. Women managers' pay rose by 6.4 per cent compared to the 5.4 per cent rise their male colleagues received. The latest survey shows that female directors received almost treble the pay increases of their male peers – a 16.2 per cent salary rise compared to 5.6 per cent.

The average woman manager earns around £33,000 – about £3,000 less than her male colleagues. Considering women managers are on average seven years younger and have worked with their employer five years less, the survey does not indicate much of a pay discrepancy between male and female managers.

> ### Women have really made their mark in the public sector where they occupy just over 40 per cent (41.5 per cent) of managerial roles

Christine Hayhurst, director of public affairs at the Institute of Management, commented: 'It is encouraging to see that women's talents are being recognised and rewarded in Britain's businesses and boardrooms. Women now make up half of today's workforce and female managers have now almost redressed pay inequalities.

However, women are under half-way to fulfilling their quota of management roles, of which they hold 22 per cent.'

For the first time in the survey's 27-year history, at least one woman sits on a board in each of the ten industry groups. Female managers have also gained ground, holding at least ten per cent of the top jobs in all industries, except engineering. Women have really made their mark in the public sector where they occupy just over 40 per cent (41.5 per cent) of managerial roles. In the financial and business services, almost a third (31.1 per cent) of managers are women.

By function, women managers in personnel are a 60 per cent majority. The actuarial, insurance and pensions group has also opened up to women, where they have over a half (54 per cent) of management positions.

The highest earning jobs for women are in IT/management services or research and development, with average salaries of just over £39,000. Finance and marketing follow, where women earn close on £37,000.

© *Institute of Management (IM)*

Female executives

According to the National Management Salary Survey 2000, released by the Institute of Management (IM) and Remuneration Economics, almost a quarter (22 per cent) of managers today are women – a great leap from only 8 per cent in 1990.

Percentage of female executives by responsibility level

Responsibility level	1990	1995	1996	1997	1998	1999	2000
Director	1.6	3.0	3.3	4.5	3.6	6.1	9.6
Function Head	4.4	5.8	6.5	8.3	10.7	11.0	15.0
Department Head	7.8	9.7	12.2	14.0	16.2	16.9	19.0
Section Leader	13.3	14.2	14.4	18.2	21.9	24.9	26.5
All Executives	7.9	10.7	12.3	15.2	18.0	19.9	22.1

Source: The Institute of Management (IM)

Managing perfectly

Women make the best bosses say the men at the top

Women make the best managers, a workplace survey has found.

And it seems their male colleagues are only too ready to agree.

Researchers found that male managers regarded their female counterparts as better with customers and more understanding of their colleagues.

They were also seen as more trustworthy, efficient and generous, the survey of 1,000 managers found.

The communication-based management style commonly adopted by women was better suited to the team approach favoured by most modern offices.

They were also likely to work hard on establishing positive relationships with staff.

Additional research showed that women scored better than men in 38 out of 47 measured management attributes.

Despite this, there are still relatively few women in senior management positions.

Although women make almost half the workforce and the intake of British universities, only 13 per cent of managers and 7 per cent of executives are female.

Sheila Coules, who chairs the social and employment issues group of the National Council of Women of Great Britain, said women's homemaking skills helped them excel at the office.

'Women have always been good at running the home as well as keeping a job which makes them good at juggling things and dealing with people,' she said.

They are generally less competitive and just want to get the job done. Also they are much better at working as a team, rather than individually, which brings a certain balance to the workplace.

'The situation with regard to women in high management positions has become stagnant recently. However, a lot of women will only apply for a job they think they are qualified for, rather than a man who will just go for anything regardless.

'Women are a tremendous resource and it is wonderful they are being recognised for this.'

'Women have always been good at running the home as well as keeping a job which makes them good at juggling things and dealing with people'

The survey results, published in *Management Today*, show that the workplace battle of the sexes may have settled down into a desire simply to ensure the best people get the best jobs.

Most managers displayed 'gender blindness' when it came to who they preferred to work with.

They did not express any particular desire to work with managers of the same sex.

Of the men surveyed, only 17 per cent said they would rather work for a male boss. Of this group, many were over 40.

Their view was shared by a mere 7 per cent of female managers.

Many of the women managers surveyed listed their male colleagues' dominant characteristics as insensitivity and more positively, decisiveness.

Men were generally regarded as not being open-minded enough or considerate.

These, however, were the very characteristics they valued in their female colleagues.

Susan Voorhees, managing director of global securitised finance with the Chase Manhattan Bank, said she had not had the luxury of preference in terms of who she would prefer as a boss.

She dismissed gender as a significant factor.

'I have never worked for a female boss so I could not comment on who I find preferable,' she said.

'However, I would look for good characteristics in a boss rather than anything gender-specific.

'Without sex stereotyping I think women do tend to empathise more and are a little less cut and dried about the way they express things and make decisions.

'I think these type of qualities tend to be attributed more to women. It is a little over simplistic to attribute these qualities to one gender.

'But I think managers in the report have probably tried to attribute certain qualities to the different genders in a positive way.'

Case study

Sara Weller is one of the few women who have made it to the top in the male-dominated arena of British retailing.

She joined Sainsbury's at the beginning of the year as the marketing supremo charged with restoring the chain to its once top position in the supermarket league.

After 13 years at Mars and a three-year stint at Abbey National, the 39-year-old executive caught the eye of Sainsbury's chiefs to land what must be one of the toughest jobs in marketing.

'I think women have different skills from men,' she said.

'They are better teamworkers and more concerned about getting the job done and less about the politics.

'Also women are often juggling other commitments so you get people who are very focused and efficient in the working hours because they have a lot to fit in around it.'

Married with a seven-year-old daughter and four-year-old son, Mrs Weller also believes women may be better communicators. 'They can put their egos to one side and work together to find solutions. This is certainly something you see more of in women than men.

'Women are equally as competitive, but competitive on the basis of the quality of what they do.

'They tend to be more concerned about being judged by results, not what they say or seem to be doing.'

Her gender is a factor in the way she approaches her job, but she prefers not to overstate its significance.

'Obviously it's part of my personality and what I do is coloured by that,' she said.

'I am also the mother of two children and, like all working mothers, I am permanently juggling things.'

Although more women are reaching director level, Mrs Weller believes it unlikely an even share of the top jobs will soon be on the agenda.

'Younger woman are starting to see older women as role models, and it should be a rolling stone with more and more people getting top jobs,' she said. 'But it will need a few successes to generate the role models.'

© The Daily Mail, 2000

Men, silent victims of sex discrimination

F amily men are among the chief victims of sexual discrimination, according to the head of the Equal Opportunities Commission.

Julie Mellor says laws should be drawn up to protect British men suffering in silence under the 'long-hours culture' which makes them the unhappiest and most stressed-out workers in Europe.

She believes male workers have been resentfully eyeing the string of tribunal awards paid recently to mothers complaining about combining parenthood with a demanding job.

Miss Mellor told *The Times* yesterday: 'Men look at what women have achieved and they would like the same thing – more part-time work, more flexible hours. But the long-hours culture prevents them even thinking about it.'

Miss Mellor would like to see the 1975 Sex Discrimination Act amended to give men as well as

By Steve Doughty, Social Affairs Correspondent

women the legal right to challenge 'indirect' discrimination.

This would enable them to bring claims for shorter hours and more time with their families to industrial tribunals.

The comments may herald an EOC campaign to give men more time off, which would at the same time offer mothers a better chance of

'Men look at what women have achieved and they would like the same thing – more part-time work, more flexible hours'

promotion as they would no longer be working fewer hours than men.

The 1975 Sex Discrimination Act makes it unlawful for employers to practice 'indirect' discrimination – rules which apply to everyone but in practice work mainly against one sex.

For example, a rule insisting that all staff be over 6ft would discriminate against women, and a rule that says all employees must work full-time would discriminate against parents of young children.

Men might, however, be able to complain that companies are over-turning practices to allow flexible working hours to mothers but are not extending the same benefit to fathers.

Miss Mellor said: 'I have always said that the last chapter in the book on feminism should be written by men.' Critics said that such claims would cost businesses billions.

© The Daily Mail, 2000

Pressure mounts for paid paternity leave

By Rachel Spence

Paternity leave is the answer to working mothers' prayers. That's the message in a controversial new report from the Industrial Society. In *Mothers vs Men: Why Women Lose at Work*, author Richard Reeves argues that it is because women are expected to shoulder the burden of childcare that, 30 years after the Equal Pay Act came into force, they still earn on average 20 per cent less than men.

'First, maternity leave entails a drop in earnings. Second, mothers often return part-time which spoils their chance of promotion. Third, some employers prefer to promote men to senior positions because they fear women may become pregnant in the future,' says Mr Reeves, who has worked out that the average woman loses £140,000 of lifetime earnings as a result of becoming a mother.

Current rules entitle both parents to three months' unpaid leave before the child is five. Mr Reeves argues that even if payment was introduced, this would do nothing to equalise the imbalance between sexes. 'However, matching paternity to maternity leave – 44 weeks, with 26 unpaid – gives both parents the potential to be equally involved in childcare, so employers are less likely to discriminate against either.'

But Ruth Lea, head of policy at the Institute of Directors, doesn't think this idea would work: 'It would disrupt smaller businesses, which struggle to accommodate maternity leave. Our members already tell us how hard it is to cover for staff.'

There's also the problem of cost. The Industrial Society suggests that, like maternity leave, it should be spread between business and taxpayer. '[It would cost] no more than £1bn per annum – a significant sum,' says the society, 'but a bargain-basement price for a social revolution.'

David Hands, spokesperson at the Federation of Small Businesses, disagrees: 'To meet the extra cost of paternity leave, many small employers would just employ less people. '

In response to these objections, Mr Reeves says: 'You have to remember that all new legislation, from married women's right to work to the minimum wage, is opposed on the grounds that business will collapse. But miraculously capitalism continues.'

Mr Reeves believes that to encourage men to take up the opportunity, paternity leave must be based on a percentage of salary, like its maternity counterpart. 'Proposals for paid parental leave call for a flat rate which, unless it's set very high, will only help low-paid men. But it's only if senior managers have an incentive to take it that the overall workplace culture will change . . . If bosses can afford to set a precedent, other men will follow.'

However, a new survey by employment agency Adecco seems to contradict this hope, with 25 per cent of men claiming to feel that taking parental leave would damage their careers. And companies such as Unilever, which introduced career breaks for all staff, have found the take-up to be much higher among women than men.

Jack O'Sullivan, spokesperson at lobbying organisation Fathers Direct, explains: 'Men find it hard to let go of traditional notions of masculinity. And they are not praised for being carers.' And although he wants to see paid parental leave for fathers, even he has reservations about equalising entitlements: 'Mothers need blocks of time off for breastfeeding and men don't. Fathers may prefer to take one day a week off, or work five-hour days. The Industrial Society's paternity leave package sounds too inflexible.'

In Sweden, both parents are entitled to 12 months' paid leave to be taken between them as they choose, plus a 'use it or lose it month' only for fathers. The leave is flexible, allowing parents to work part-time if they wish, and there is a high take-up rate.

In the UK, advertising agency Howell Henry Chaldecott Lury has taken some lessons from Scandinavia. 'Currently, we offer two weeks' paid paternity leave and three-to-six-month career breaks for everyone,' says human resources director Lou Burrows.

Contradicting those who say hands-on fathers are bad for business, he adds: 'We're beginning to see that the flexibility we offer gives us an edge over our competitors. We've just hired an incredibly talented senior strategic planner without paying him a higher salary. He chose to come here because he wanted to spend more time with his children and he knew we'd give him that freedom.'

© *Independent Newspapers Ltd, 2000*

ADDITIONAL RESOURCES

You might like to contact the following organisations for further information. Due to the increasing cost of postage, many organisations cannot respond to enquiries unless they receive a stamped, addressed envelope.

Equal Opportunities Commission (EOC)
Arndale House
Arndale Centre
Manchester, M4 3EQ
Tel: 0161 833 9244
Fax: 0161 835 1657
E-mail: info@eoc.org.uk
Web site: www.eoc.org.uk
Works toward the elimination of unlawful sex and marriage discrimination, to promote equality of opportunities between women and men generally and to keep the Sex Discrimination Act and Equal Pay Act under review.

Equal Opportunities Commission – Scotland
St Stephen's House
279 Bath Street
Glasgow
Scotland, G2 4JL
Tel: 0141 248 5833
Fax: 0141 248 5834
E-mail: scotland@eoc.org.uk
Web site: www.eoc.org.uk
The Equal Opportunities Commission has three main tasks: working to end sex discrimination, promoting equal opportunities for women and men, and reviewing and suggesting improvements to the Sexual Discrimination Act and the Equal Pay Act.

Fawcett Society
5th Floor
45 Beech Street
London, EC2Y 8AD
Tel: 020 7628 4441
Fax: 020 7628 2865
E-mail: fawcett@gn.apc.org.uk
Web site: www.gn.apc.org/fawcett
Works to influence public opinion to accept equal status for women in the home and public life, and equal educational and job opportunities. Publishes *Towards Equality*, a quarterly publication. To subscribe to *Towards Equality* and other publications send £25.00 to: Fawcett Society, Freepost FE 6903, London, EC2B 2JD.

Joseph Rowntree Foundation (JRF)
The Homestead
40 Water End
York
North Yorkshire, YO30 6WP
Tel: 01904 629241
Fax: 01904 620072
E-mail: infor@jrf.org.uk
Web site: www.jrf.org.uk
The Foundation is an independent, non-political body which funds programmes of research and innovative development in the fields of housing, social care and social policy. It publishes its research findings rapidly and widely so that they can inform current debate and practice.

National Family and Parenting Institute (NFPI)
430 Highgate Studios
58-79 Highgate Road
London, NW5 1TL
Tel: 020 7424 3460
Fax: 020 7424 3590
E-mail: info@nfpi.org
Web site: www.nfpi.org
The Institute's role is to bring together organisations, knowledge and know-how to enhance the value and quality of family life, to make sure that parents are supported in bringing up their children and in finding the help and information they need.

The Future Foundation
First Floor
14-16 Cowcross Street
London, EC1M 6DG
Tel: 020 7250 3343
Fax: 020 7251 8138
E-mail: info@futurefoundation.net
Web site: www.futurefoundation.net
The Future Foundation is a business focused think-tank set up in July 1996 which aims to help organisations improve their performance through understanding, anticipating and responding to their customers.

The Industrial Society
Customer Centre
49 Calthorpe Road
Edgbaston, Birmingham, B15 1TH
Tel: 01870 400 1000
Fax: 01780 400 1099
E-mail: customercentre@indsoc.co.uk
Web site: www.indsoc.co.uk
The Industrial Society is an independent, not-for-profit campaigning body with over 10,000 member organisations from every part of the economy.

The Institute of Management
3rd Floor, 2 Savoy Court
Strand, London, WC2R 0EZ
Tel: 020 7497 0580
Fax: 020 7497 0463
Web site: www.inst-mgt.org.uk
The Institute of Management represents around 86,000 individual managers making it the largest broadly based management institute in the UK.

Trades Union Congress – Equal Rights Department (TUC)
Congress House
23-28 Great Russell Street
London, WC1B 3LS
Tel: 020 7636 4030
Fax: 020 7636 0632
E-mail: info@tuc.org.uk
Web site: www.tuc.org.uk
The TUC has over 75 member trade unions, representing nearly seven million people from all walks of life. They campaign on concerns in the world of work and build links with all political parties, business and the community.

United Kingdom Men's Movement
P.O. Box 205
Cheltenham, GL51 0YL
Tel: 01242 691110
Web site: www.ukmm.org.uk
The United Kingdom Men's Movement wishes to protect the equitable rights of men. They invite all men and women to help them in the restoration of our decaying society.

*****

The Internet has been likened to shopping in a supermarket without aisles. The press of a button on a Web browser can bring up thousands of sites but working your way through them to find what you want can involve long and frustrating on-line searches.

And unfortunately many sites contain inaccurate, misleading or heavily biased information. Our researchers have therefore undertaken an extensive analysis to bring you a selection of quality Web site addresses.

Equal Opportunities Commission (EOC)
www.eoc.org.uk
The Equal Opportunities Commission is the expert body on equality between women and men. Its site provides a comprehensive coverage of equal opportunity issues.

Fawcett Society
www.gn.apc.org/fawcett
Fawcett campaigns for equality between women and men. This site looks at women's daily experience in the workplace, in politics and in retirement.

UK Men and Father's Rights
www.coeffic.demon.co.uk/index.htm
Puts the case for men's rights claiming it is men rather than women who are the real victims of sexual discrimination. This site contain thought-provoking articles which are sure to stimulate debate.

United Kingdom Men's Movement
www.ukmm.org.uk
United Kingdom Men's Movement campaigns for a fair deal for men. It looks at issues of fundamental importance for men's lives and for our society.

Trades Union Congress (TUC)
www.tuc.org.uk
The 'Fair Pay for Women Now!' campaign was launched at the TUC Women's Conference in March 2000. Visit their site for more details.

ACKNOWLEDGEMENTS

The publisher is grateful for permission to reproduce the following material.

While every care has been taken to trace and acknowledge copyright, the publisher tenders its apology for any accidental infringement or where copyright has proved untraceable. The publisher would be pleased to come to a suitable arrangement in any such case with the rightful owner.

Chapter One: Equality in Schools

Equality issues in education, © Equal Opportunities Commission (EOC), *Pupils achieving 5 or more GCSE grade A*–C*, © Crown copyright is reproduced with the permission of the Controller of Her Majesty's Stationery Office, *Young women and education*, © European Women's Lobby (EWL), *Girls take top grades in most subjects*, © Guardian Newspapers Limited 2000, *The mark of the male*, © Dr Anthony Grayling, *Gender stereotypes still hamper young*, © Guardian Newspapers Limited 2000, *The law on sex discrimination in education*, © Equal Opportunities Commission – Scotland, *Gender and education*, © Equal Opportunities Commission (EOC), *Pupils achieving GCSE grade A–C*: by selected subject and gender*, © Crown copyright is reproduced with the permission of the Controller of Her Majesty's Stationery Office.

Chapter Two: Equality in the Home

Battle of sexes set for truce, © The Future Foundation, *Women in the UK*, © The Future Foundation, *Mind the pay gap*, © Crown copyright is reproduced with the permission of the Controller of Her Majesty's Stationery Office, *Background situation*, © The United Kingdom Men's Movement, *Changing gender relationships*, © European Women's Lobby (EWL), *Economic activity status of women*, © Labour Force Survey, Office of National Statistics, *Waddaya mean,*

the war's over?, © Guardian Newspapers Limited 2000, *Why the future belongs to women*, © The Daily Mail, 2000, *A man's place in the home*, © Joseph Rowntree Foundation, *Daddy's home . . .* , © Guardian Newspapers Limited 2000, *The world's women 2000*, © United Nations (New York, Department of Economic and Social Affairs, Statistics Division).

Chapter Three: Equality in the Workplace

Work and the family today, © The National Family and Parenting Institute, *The work-life balance*, © Equal Opportunities Commission (EOC), *Sex discrimination*, © The Industrial Society, *Fair pay for women now!*, © Trades Union Congress (TUC), *Mothers versus men*, © The Industrial Society, 2000, *Will women always be second in the workplace?*, © Ruth Lea and Richard Reeves, *Valuing women*, © Equal Opportunities Commission (EOC), *Fair pay for women workers*, © Trades Union Congress (TUC), *Young people's attitudes to, and awareness of, equal pay*, © Equal Opportunities Commission (EOC), *The gender pay gap*, © Equal Opportunities Commission (EOC), *Equal pay and low pay campaign*, © The Fawcett Society, *Women make inroads into top jobs*, © The Institute of Management (IM), *Female Executives*, © The Institute of Management (IM), *Managing perfectly*, © The Daily Mail, 2000, *Men, silent victims of sex discrimination*, © The Daily Mail, 2000, *Pressure mounts for paid paternity leave*, © Independent Newspapers Ltd, 2000.

Photographs and illustrations:

Pages 1, 5, 13, 20, 26, 30, 38: Simon Kneebone, 9, 15, 18, 24: Pumpkin House.

Craig Donnellan
Cambridge
January, 2001